SPECIAL EatingW

# EATING FOR STRENGTH

Why Stronger Is Better • How to Eat Protein Now
The Perfect Foods • Stay Strong for Life

# Contents



Parts of this special edition were previously published by *EatingWell, Health* and *Shape*.

There are two covers of this *EatingWell* special edition.

INTRODUCTION

# GETTING STRONGER, LIVING BETTER

Adding strength training to your life can invite a myriad of health benefits, ranging from a healthier heart to a sunnier outlook.

**BY JOYCE HENDLEY**

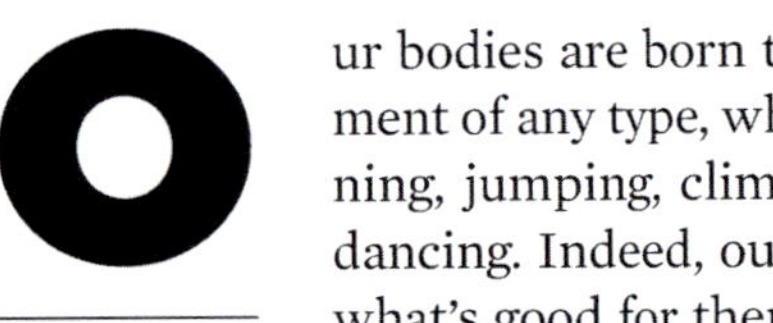

Our bodies are born to crave movement of any type, whether it's running, jumping, climbing a tree or dancing. Indeed, our bodies know what's good for them. These days, research seems to uncover a new, breathtaking benefit of exercise for our health almost daily, whether it's helping us live longer, sleep better, weigh less or even feel happier.

We've long known that it's critical to get in regular aerobic, or cardio, workouts like running, biking, brisk walking or swimming—those activities that cause us to get out of breath and make our hearts beat faster. But just as important is regularly doing exercises that strengthen our muscles, including strength and resistance training. These activities, from lifting weights or doing push-ups to using resistance bands or kettlebells, help keep our muscles functioning, supporting all the activities of our daily lives. And their longevity-boosting, age-fighting effects help make fitness the closest thing we have to a fountain of youth.

Muscle strengthening has benefits for everyone, from body builders to octogenarians. In fact, any time is a good time to start. Research has demonstrated that even people in their 80s and 90s benefit from strength and resistance training, gaining better mobility, experiencing fewer falls and enjoying an improved quality of life overall. No matter where you're at physically or how old you are, it's

clear that adding more strength training into your life will boost your health and fitness, and make your life better. It's just that simple.

But what are strength and resistance training, exactly? Both are part of what the U.S. Physical Activity Guidelines define as "muscle-strengthening exercises"—those designed to improve muscle strength, tone, mass and endurance by causing the body's muscles to work or hold against an applied force or weight. While muscle strengthening exercise is usually associated with lifting weights or other heavy objects, it also includes working with resistance bands, cable suspension training or even exercises that use your own weight to generate the resistance, such as push-ups and pull-ups, lunges, even tree climbing. The idea is to progressively overload your muscles, strengthening them and helping them work more efficiently. Plus, the foods that promote muscle development and contribute to recovery are healthful and nutrient-dense.

And, while you might be picturing a ripped, Incredible Hulk-esque man or woman lifting giant barbells, strength training doesn't have to mean "bulking up" at all. Would-be Hulks need to train

heavily and adapt their diet to boost significant muscle growth—a process that requires a lot of time, energy and commitment. But for the rest of us, strength training is more about spending a few sessions a week creating a solid, muscular base of lean body mass that burns more calories and makes everyday activities easier.

Best of all, strength training is easy to work into your life. You don't have to go to a gym, and you don't need to make expensive equipment investments. It need not take more than a couple dumbbells or weights, a set of resistance bands, a exercise ball or kettlebell, or even using what you have on hand (cans of food, say). And unless you're aiming for Hulk status, the time investment is manageable: the U.S. Physical Activity Guidelines for Americans recommend doing a strength training workout just two to three times a week (along with at least 150 minutes of moderate-intensity or 75 minutes of vigorous aerobic activity.

The investment in making your body stronger might be relatively small, but the gains are powerful. Here's a roundup of what the latest science shows about what strength training can offer you.

### A Leaner, Stronger Body

And maybe a flatter belly, too. With consistent strength training, your muscles will become more dense—which can help you burn more calories and better manage your weight. In one study that put 40 men and women on a six-month program of weight training, researchers found that participants' resting metabolic rate—the rate at which they burned calories all day long—increased, on average, by 7 percent. And, though the evidence is still not definitive, some research suggests that strength training is associated with less accumulation of "belly fat"—the visceral fat around the abdomen that's associated with higher rates of diabetes, inflammation, and risk of heart disease.

### Better Bone and Muscle Health

Strength training workouts can also have benefits for bones, as muscles and tendons pull on and put stress on them, spurring bone-forming cells to become more active. That can result in stronger, denser bones, building up a stronger bank of bone tissue that can help delay or prevent osteoporosis later in life. Staying active can help stave off or even reverse the effects of sarcopenia—the slow muscle loss that occurs with aging. It's estimated that after age 30 or so, if we don't remain active, we can lose 3 to 5 percent of our muscle mass per decade—which, by the time we reach our 70s, can result in problems like slowed gait, falls, fractures and other scourges we associate with getting older.

### A Healthier Heart

Weight training can help your heart in several important ways, starting with its effects on helping you manage your weight. With a leaner body, your heart has less work to do and pumps more efficiently. Weight training can also improve overall circulation, as your muscles become more efficient at pushing blood through your veins and arteries, further reducing strain on your heart. Research confirms the benefits: A recent study from Iowa State University that looked at data from 13,000 adults found that those who included at least one weekly session of weight training (or accumulated up to an hour per week of weight training) had a significantly lower risk of heart attack and stroke, as well as death from any cause.

### Better Blood-Sugar Management

Research shows that strength training can have important effects on helping people with diabetes or insulin resistance better manage their blood sugar levels. Besides increasing the amount of metabolically active, glucose-fueled muscle tissue, strength training appears to boost muscles' ability to take in glucose from the blood, resulting in lower blood sugar levels overall.

### Better Joint Health

Strength training can help improve how your muscles cushion your joints, which can help manage joint pain and stiffness. One meta-analysis of 10 studies, published in the journal *Rheumatology*, reported that strengthening the muscle groups around troublesome joints significantly improved strength and functioning, and eased pain in people with osteoarthritis. And, of course, if you're overweight, the training could help you lose a few pounds, resulting in less stress on your joints overall. (Note: If you have arthritis or other joint issues, make sure you clear any exercise program first with your doctor or physical therapist, to make sure you're doing it safely.)

### Better Sleep, More Energy

Several studies show that regular strength workouts can improve sleep—helping you fall asleep faster and wake up less during the night. Recently published findings from the German Health Update Survey, which tracked the health of some 23,000 German adults, found that those who regularly practiced strength training reported significantly better sleep quality. It's also true that better sleep can go a long way toward improving your overall health and energy levels. As you grow stronger, you'll find everyday activities like carrying groceries or laundry are easier to do, and you won't be as fatigued in general.

### More Happiness

The so-called "runner's high" isn't just for runners and other cardio exercisers: Strength training has also been shown to help the body release feel-good endorphins that enhance your sense of well-being. That can help take the edge off your worries and anxieties, as a recent study of 28 young adults with generalized anxiety disorder suggests. After two months of a twice-weekly resistance exercise program, subjects tested significantly lower on anxiety-symptom scales than a similar control group who didn't get the exercise intervention. There may be positive effects in fighting depression as well: One 2018 review of 33 clinical trials found that adults who regularly strength trained were less likely to develop depression than those who didn't. What's more, there's an indefinable boost in confidence as your body reaches measurable fitness goals and crushes them. You'll find yourself moving more confidently and freely—and that can have positive effects on your mood and outlook, too.

**Strength training is about spending a few sessions a week on creating a solid, muscular base of lean body mass that burns more calories and makes everyday activities easier.**

It's easy to start adding strength training to your life right now, no matter where you are. And when it comes to the results, it's all good. Go at your own pace and feel the benefits unfold, faster than you might imagine. And as with all exercise, the benefits keep accruing. Better health, increased energy, more enthusiasm and more confidence are all within your reach. Grab your weights or resistance bands—or just some comfortable clothes—and let's get started! ●

CHAPTER 1

# FOODS THAT FUEL

These nutrient-dense meals and tips will feed your health and improve your workouts.

# PRINCIPLES OF STRENGTH

Adding healthful ingredients into your diet and balancing sources of protein, carbs and fat can help maximize returns on time spent working out. Plus, secrets that can give you an added edge.

**BY ASHLEY ABRAMSON**

Imagine you have a brick wall in your backyard. It's functional enough, but you've got your sights set on replacing it with a larger, stronger one. Before you grab your sledgehammer and start knocking down the bricks, you need to make a plan. You know that to build a stronger wall, you'll have to tear down the old one first, but that's only part of the process. You'll also need the right tools to rebuild a bigger, better and stronger wall in its place.

Building muscle is a similar process, says Jeff Lucchino, RDN, director of sports nutrition at University of Pittsburgh Medical Center Sports Medicine. Challenging your muscles with resistance training can cause your muscle fibers to break down and rebuild, a process called hypertrophy. But resistance training is only one part of the equation. You also need to give your body the tools it needs to power through that workout, to effectively rebuild muscle after it and to recover after your hard work.

You may already know that building strength has plenty of health benefits. According to a 2015 paper in the *American College of Sports Medicine Health & Fitness Journal,* resistance training can improve bone density, insulin sensitivity, cholesterol levels and cognitive ability along with decreasing body fat, blood pressure, low-back pain and depression.

While many types of strength training can increase muscle size, one form stands above the rest if you want to get stronger, too. In a 2021 meta-analysis published in *Medicine & Science in Sports & Exercise,* researchers found that people who lifted higher loads with more frequency improved their strength more than people who didn't. In other words, frequency and intensity both play a role in building strength.

TIMING CERTAIN MEALS TO YOUR WORKOUTS CAN GIVE YOU AN ADDED EDGE.

OATMEAL IS A HEALTHY CARB THAT'S HIGH IN FIBER. BE SURE TO EAT IT AT LEAST AN HOUR BEFORE YOUR WORKOUT TO AVOID DIGESTIVE WOES.

If you're lifting light weights a few times a week, you likely don't need to change your nutritional approach, much like you don't need to guzzle down a protein drink every time you go on a 30-minute walk. But those who do more intense daily or near-daily strength work can increase their results by considering evidence-backed principles of nutrition for building and sustaining muscle.

As beneficial as strength building can be, strengthening muscles (and reaping the health benefits of doing so) takes time and strategy. Ryan Andrews, a principal nutritionist and adviser for Precision Nutrition and an adjunct instructor at Purchase College, State University of New York, says he always reminds his clients that doing more intense weight training triggers important metabolic changes in the body.

"They're breaking down and damaging muscles, and those muscles need repair," Andrews says. "But they're also producing more energy, circulating oxygen, putting stress on their bones and connective tissue, and demanding more from their brain." To assist the body in all this activity—not to mention building bigger, stronger, muscles—requires incorporating the right nutrients into your routine as well. "Someone can have the most immaculate weight-lifting routine, but that's only part of the process," Andrews notes.

Here's what you need to know about streamlining your nutrition for strength training, according to researchers and nutritionists.

### First, Work Out Often

Before you drastically switch up your diet, commit to your exercise regimen. While many factors can make weight lifting more effective, spending time working your muscles is the most important ingredient. "No amount of nutrition or supplements will ever make up for not going to the gym," says Stuart Phillips, PhD, professor of kinesiology at McMaster University in Hamilton, Ontario. "That's going to drive about 80 to 90 percent of what you see in terms of strength and muscle mass gains and fat loss. You just can't get around that."

Hypertrophy, the tearing and rebuilding of muscle tissue, only happens when you continually challenge yourself. Your body will adapt to what you're lifting, so you must consistently increase the weight. (Muscles also adapt to the same exercises.) Eric Helms, PhD, research fellow at Sports Performance Research Institute New Zealand, says growing muscle tissue requires disrupting homeostasis. "If you want to keep making progress over time, you have to lift heavier weights," he says. "If you're not doing that, there's no muscle protein breakdown, and there's no reason to emphasize nutrition."

### Consider Your Calorie Intake

Once you've committed to a challenging, consistent weight-training program, it's time to make a few key changes to your diet. If you're looking to lose weight, strength training is a great way to burn fat and encourage your body to burn more calories throughout the day. And Phillips says women who lose weight when they strength train are more likely to lose fat mass versus muscle mass, which is beneficial for overall health.

To lose weight, you'll need to be in a calorie deficit, which means consuming fewer calories per day than you need, burning more calories through exercise than you eat or a combination of both. You may wind up eating more than you did before to fuel yourself for exercise, but as long as you're in a deficit, Phillips says, you should still shed pounds.

If your goal is to build larger, stronger muscles, you'll definitely need to eat more. "You'll only grow so much if you don't consume more energy, so plan to be in a calorie surplus," says Helms. There's no specific formula for calorie intake. The important thing, he says, is to make sure you're eating enough to slowly gain weight. Start by tracking what you're eating in a calorie app. If you aren't gaining weight, try increasing your intake by 100 to 200 calories a day until you reach a level of weight gain you're satisfied with.

The only caveat to boosting your calorie intake: If you're just starting a serious resistance training routine and you want to lose weight, your body can use the fat you already have for energy during workouts. For example, Helms says, if you're 20 pounds heavier than you want to be, you can make progress losing those 20 pounds and building muscle without eating more. That's because when you start lifting weights, there's a much lower threshold for adaptation. Once you lose the weight, though, you may struggle to keep putting on muscle—so you'll need to boost your calorie intake.

After you land on the calorie excess that works best for you, Helms says, you can focus on incorporating the right macronutrients into your diet.

### Energize with Carbohydrates

In order to do exercises that build strength—or engage in any workout, for that matter—you'll need energy in the form of carbohydrates, says Nancy Clark, RD, a sports nutritionist and the author of *Nancy Clark's Sports Nutrition Guidebook*. Resistance training requires energy; lifting heavy weights, Clark says, can quickly deplete stored glycogen, or stored carbohydrates. "When we eat carbohydrates, they get broken down into glucose, which gets stored in your muscles as glycogen," she explains. "So if you're lifting weights, you'll need a little more of that fuel."

According to Clark, any fruit, vegetable or grain can be an effective source of muscle fuel, but as you know, junk food won't improve your overall health. For instance, a Reese's Peanut Butter Cup could effectively fuel your muscles for a resistance training workout, but a banana with peanut butter on it offers carbohydrates, plus the fat, protein and micronutrients you need to build muscle and improve your health in general.

Exactly how many carbs should someone who takes strength training seriously be consuming? While you probably won't need as much carb fuel as a track athlete, Phillips suggests aiming for about 200 to 300 grams of complex carbohydrates each day. Focusing on increasing calories while boosting your overall nutrient intake. Whole grains, such as whole grain bread, oatmeal, quinoa, barley, beans and sweet potatoes, contain plenty of carbs along with other nutrients to boost your overall health.

A high-fiber snack will take longer to digest and draw blood to your digestive system, which can make you feel full and slow down your workout. So before you you exercise, aim to eat carbs that aren't extremely high in fiber, such as pasta, crackers, cereal or bread that's not enriched with fiber. If your primary goal is weight loss, you'll still need the same fuel as someone who wants to build muscle—just pay attention to portion size so you don't end up with a calorie excess. "Eat to the point of mild satiety rather than the point where you're so full you can't move," Phillips says.

When you eat your carbohydrates matters, too. If you're looking for an extra edge, Lucchino recommends consuming a carb-rich meal about three or so hours before you do your workout, then grabbing a carb-rich snack—such as a granola bar with 8 to 10 grams of protein and 20 grams of carbs, or a piece of toast with peanut butter on it—about an hour before.

Clark suggests incorporating a similar carbohydrate-rich food in your post-workout protein snack. Studies show that eating carbs after resistance exercise can help the body restore its supply of muscle glycogen, which could facilitate faster recovery, and, in the long run, a greater training volume.

## Rebuild with Protein

Working your muscles tears them apart, so to build them, you'll need to eat nutrients that help your muscle fibers repair themselves—think of protein as the mortar you'd use to rebuild the brick wall you had knocked down. Protein is made up of building blocks called amino acids, which help repair and rebuild broken-down muscle tissue after a workout. "Eating protein throughout the day helps repair that muscle tissue and get it ready for the next strength-training workout," Lucchino says.

If you're lifting weights several times a week, you'll need to consume more protein, even if you want to lose weight. In addition to helping build muscle (so you can burn fat), protein is more satiating, so it'll keep you feeling full more than other nutrients. Ultimately, how much protein you should eat depends on how much you weigh. The Dietary Reference Intake suggests 0.36 grams of protein per day per pound of body fat—for a 140-pound person, that comes to 150 grams of protein each day. But Phillips says anyone who strength trains seriously might need more than that.

"Throughout the day, you want to get the most bang for your buck," Clark points out. "So if your goal is to lose weight, choose high-protein foods that are lower in calories." She recommends, for example, eggs, low-fat cottage cheese, chicken, lean pork and tuna.

If you want to add muscle bulk, Helms suggests eating 0.7 to 1 grams of protein per pound of your current body weight. If you weigh 170 pounds, you would want to aim for a daily amount of about 119 to 170 grams of protein.

Try to spread your protein throughout the day, incorporating lean meats, eggs, legumes, nuts and dairy into your meals and snacks. Helms suggests three larger servings of protein spread out through your three meals, along with one or two protein-rich snacks, to reach your target. Or, Lucchino says, you could plan to consume protein every three to five hours (not counting overnight, since you are not eating then).

For an added boost, consume protein around the time you train as a way to encourage muscle recovery—plan a protein-heavy snack for one or two hours before and after your workout. Lucchino suggests packing a quick and convenient snack for the gym, such as a handful of nuts or slices of cheese. Another alternative might be a homemade shake with protein powder, Greek yogurt, almond milk, and a banana. Choose protein powders that have gone through third-party testing to ensure the product is what the manufacturer says it is.

When it comes to protein sources, keep quality in mind. If your primary goal is to gain muscle, you can technically do that with any type of protein. But if you don't want to put on body mass, consider your protein sources carefully. For example, a fast-food burger can boost both your calories and protein, but you'll ultimately end up eating more calories than you need to reach your protein intake, which could throw off your weight-loss goals. Instead, go for lean protein paired with complex carbohydrates.

If you're serious about lifting and struggling to eat enough protein to make a difference, supplementing can help. Phillips and his colleagues found in a 2018 systematic review that supplementing protein above the normally recommended amount can enhance strength and muscle-mass gain. For building muscle, look for a protein powder that's easy for your body to absorb and use, such as whey protein or whey isolates.

## Recover with Healthy Fats

It may seem counterproductive to consume fat if you're hoping to lose fat and gain muscle, but fat is an important part of a nutritious diet. The body

needs it for energy, to form cell walls and absorb vitamins, and to protect your organs. According to the Dietary Guidelines for Americans, fats should make up between 20 and 35 percent of your total calorie intake. If you're eating more calories, you'll need more fat. If you're eating fewer calories to lose weight, you'll need less fat.

"People fear fat because they worry they'll gain fat on their body, but it definitely helps in the accumulation of lean muscle mass," Lucchino says. "You'll only gain fat if you're consuming a lot more calories than you're burning in your training."

Of course, not all fats are created equal. The best type of fat for muscle building—and overall health—is polyunsaturated fats, such as omega-3 fatty acids found in fatty fish like salmon, nuts, nut butter, seeds and oils.

Ensuring ample fat intake can also help your body absorb fat-soluble vitamins—essential nutrients that are absorbed with fat—such as vitamin D, which is important for bone and immune system health, mood, and insulin regulation. And if you're struggling to eat enough calories for any muscle-building goals, consuming more fat, which tends to be higher in calories, can help you get there.

Just avoid too much fat before a workout. Because fat can slow digestion, it can make you uncomfortable and compromise athletic performance.

## Don't Neglect Micronutrients

If you're focusing on building muscle, finding the right balance of the macronutrients protein, fat, and carbs can help you reach your goals. But micronutrients such as vitamins and minerals play an important role in priming your body for muscle growth and overall health. For example, your body needs ample iron (found in meat, beans and many breakfast cereals) to move oxygen through your system, magnesium (found in spinach and many seeds and nuts) to de-stress after an intense workout and

vitamin C (found in citrus fruits, peppers, strawberries and broccoli, to name a few) to boost bone health. Healthy vitamin D levels ensure you have the hormones you need to grow and maintain muscles. You can find vitamin D in fatty fish such as salmon and mackerel, along with egg yolks, cheese and some mushrooms. "If you're deficient in micronutrients that can help build muscle, then you're probably not going to get the most optimal return on your investment at the gym," Andrews says.

A diet rich in fruits and vegetables is one way to make sure you get all the nutrients your body needs to function optimally, Andrews adds. Focus on adding color to your meals to ensure a variety of fruits and vegetables, and when you can, eat as many whole-food sources as possible.

## Stay Hydrated

While you're at it, drink plenty of water throughout the day; studies have found that low fluid intake can impact the effectiveness of resistance-training workouts. But dehydration can also negatively impact your overall health. Your body needs water for many functions, from keeping your joints lubricated and regulating body temperature to preventing infections and delivering nutrients to your cells. You'll also sleep better and feel better when you're well hydrated, which means you'll have more energy to exercise when you want to.

There's no hard-and-fast rule about how much water you should consume. The U.S. National Academies of Sciences, Engineering and Medicine has determined that most men need about 15.5 cups of fluids a day, while women need about 11.5 cups daily. (Keep in mind that you also get fluids from other beverages and food.) As a general rule, if you don't feel thirsty and your urine is light or clear, you're probably well hydrated.

To be sure you're getting enough fluids, fill a water bottle and sip on it throughout the day, and refill it when it's empty. You may need more water if you're exercising, so pay attention to when you're feeling thirsty.

## Create Sustainable Routines

As with any goal, building stronger, healthier muscles depends on your routines. The more you strength train and incorporate nutritional principles that help your body build and retain muscle, the better results you'll see. If you get stuck in the process or need encouragement, enlist an expert. "You can get some good information from a nutritionist about what will help you most and work together to put together a plan that supports your goals," Andrews says.

That said, being too strict with your routines can take a toll on your mental health and have the opposite effect on your muscle gain and fat loss process than you intended. Instead of fussing with complicated grocery lists and obsessive macronutrient tracking, Andrews suggests building a small menu of nutrient-dense go-to meals and snacks you enjoy and can easily prepare, then rotating through them and swapping them out when you want a change.

And while Helms says it's generally healthier to eat minimally processed, single-item food ingredients, that doesn't mean you can never have dessert or go out to eat. Strategy is important in promoting any positive health outcome—but stress and rigidity won't encourage you to stick to the routine that will help you improve your health. ●

# Powered by Plants

New science shows you can build muscle without meat in your diet. Here, sports dietitians spill the beans on what you need to know.

**BY AMANDA LOUDIN**

It's no secret that interest in plant-based diets is booming. More than half of Americans are looking to curb their meat and dairy consumption and eat more produce, according to a survey from the Yale Program on Climate Change Communication. Yet many active people are concerned that going meatless (or almost meatless) won't give them enough of the complete protein they need to build muscle and recover from their workouts, says Natalie Rizzo, RD, a New York City-based dietitian who specializes in vegan and vegetarian diets for athletes.

The good news: Research suggests that plant-forward diets can be as effective—if not more so—at building strength and helping you get the best results from your efforts. Follow these tips to ensure you fuel your body right.

**MIX UP YOUR PROTEIN SOURCES**

Our bodies need protein to help repair and build muscle. And it's true that animal proteins are the most efficient sources—they have more protein per gram and contain all nine essential amino acids in adequate amounts. But you can still meet your needs with plant-based proteins. The key is variety, says sports dietitian Angie Asche, RD, owner of Eleat Sports Nutrition in Lincoln, Nebraska. Because plant proteins vary in their amino acid content, Asche recommends including lots of different nutritious sources—such as nuts, seeds, legumes and whole grains—in your diet for the best recovery.

This doesn't mean you need more protein than meat eaters, though, notes Rizzo. The American College of Sports Medicine recommends that active people aim for at least half a gram of protein per pound of body weight a day but sets the top of the range at 0.8 grams per pound. That's 75 to 120 grams if you weigh 150 pounds, which adds up quickly, considering that ½ cup chickpeas and 2 tablespoons of peanut butter each contain about 7 grams of protein.

**BALANCE YOUR RECOVERY WITH CARBS**

After a tough workout, your body goes into recuperation mode for around 24 hours, replenishing stored carbohydrates and rebuilding muscles so you're ready for your next session. "Since your body can only use so much carbohydrate and protein at a time, the goal is to eat modest amounts of both at each meal and snack to aid in recovery," says Rizzo. That could mean a post-run nibble of a piece of fruit with some nut butter or a grain bowl filled with protein-rich bulgur wheat and veggies for lunch.

**MIND THE GAPS**

As you swap animal food sources for plants, there are a few important nutrients to be aware of. Regular workouts can deplete your stores of iron and lead to fatigue. Many plants contain non-heme iron, but it's not absorbed as well as the heme variety found in animals, explains Rizzo. Adding vitamin-C-rich foods such as bell peppers and broccoli to your meals can improve iron uptake. Other nutrients you may fall short on include vitamin $B_{12}$—it's only found in animal foods, so you may consider taking a supplement—and calcium, which is in plants like soy, fortified cereals and green vegetables (think kale, bok choy and spinach). Your muscles—heck, your whole body—will thank you.

# BEST FOODS FOR STRENGTH

From plant-based proteins to lean meats, these healthy superfoods are loaded with good-for-you nutrients that help increase energy, build stronger muscles and ease workout ailments.

**BY EMILY JOSHU**

## Eggs

Eggs are a high-protein choice with versatility for every meal. Whether for breakfast in a frittata or mixed into a dinner salad, they can help build and maintain muscle. One large egg contains several B vitamins, which have been shown to be critically important for energy production. Eggs also contain large amounts of the amino acid leucine, which aids muscle growth. However, the majority of the nutrients can be found in the yolk; the egg white contains only protein. Additionally, eggs can help you feel satiated for longer. One small study in the *Journal of the American College of Nutrition* found, for example, that women who ate eggs for breakfast felt fuller longer and ate fewer calories throughout the day, which could contribute to fat loss.

## Salmon

Salmon is one of the most plentiful sources of omega-3 fatty acids, which could improve muscular health and muscle gain. One 3-ounce portion of salmon, for example, contains 2 grams of omega-3s, almost twice the recommended daily value for adults. That same portion also contains 17 grams of protein and half of the recommended daily value of selenium, a metabolism-boosting mineral that comes from food. Additionally, salmon is rich in energy-producing B vitamins, similar to eggs. These nutrients all help repair muscles, so a piece of salmon at dinner could keep muscles healthy after a tough workout.

## Greek Yogurt

Dairy products that are packed with protein could have an impact on building lasting lean muscle. Research has shown that people who consume a combination of fast- and slow-digesting dairy proteins might experience increases in lean mass. However, star probiotic Greek yogurt stands out among other dairy proteins. Greek yogurt contains

A 2018 STUDY FOUND THAT WHOLE EGGS BUILD MUSCLE FAR BETTER THAN JUST EGG WHITES.

nearly double the amount of protein as regular yogurt. This high level could help boost metabolism and keep you satiated longer than regular yogurt can. Additionally, a 2019 study in the journal *Frontiers in Nutrition* found that college-age men who consumed nonfat Greek yogurt after resistance training "increased most measures of strength, biceps muscle thickness and fat-free mass," the researchers wrote.

## Quinoa

The popular grain is a good high-protein choice—24 grams per cup—for a post-workout side dish. This superfood is also rich in magnesium, with one cup providing nearly one third of the recommended daily value, which helps promote protein synthesis. The same serving of quinoa is also packed with all nine amino acids that can be found in food, which is essential for building muscle. Because quinoa is high in carbohydrates, containing more than 39 grams per cooked cup, eat it right after a workout to aid muscle recovery.

## Milk

While milk is often associated with building healthy bones, science shows that it can also be a strong choice for muscle building. According to the American College of Sports Medicine in 2016, "milk-based protein after resistance exercise is effective in increasing muscle strength and favorable changes in body composition." A 2010 study in the journal *Medicine & Science in Sports & Exercise* found that drinking milk promotes greater lean muscle gains and improves overall strength, due to its high level

of the amino acid leucine, which aids in muscle protein synthesis. Dairy milk is also a strong source of calcium, and that assists muscle contraction, which helps build muscle during exercise.

### Bison

A lean alternative to other red meats, bison contains several essential nutrients that aid in muscle health. One 4-ounce serving contains 68 percent of the recommended daily value of vitamin $B_{12}$, as well as 19 percent of the recommended daily value of vitamin $B_6$, which can aid energy production. It also contains nearly one third of the daily recommended value of selenium, which can boost metabolism. This low-calorie choice—just 124 calories per 4-ounce serving—also has a mild taste, which makes it a lean swap for beef or other red meats.

### Avocados

Touted as an all-encompassing superfood, avocados are packed with 20 essential vitamins and minerals that can help keep muscles healthy. Avocados are rich in vitamins $B_5$, $B_6$, C, E and K, as well as potassium and folate. They contain about 20 percent of the recommended daily value of folate, a B vitamin that helps convert carbohydrates into energy, which makes them an essential pre- and post-workout pick. They also contain about 14 percent of the daily recommended value of potassium, a mineral that helps regulate fluid balance and muscle contractions. Additionally, avocados are rich in fiber, which helps the body stay satiated for longer, supporting weight loss.

### Bananas

Bananas are an easy and convenient snack. Because they are rich in water and carbs—27 grams in one medium banana—research has shown that they can improve exercise performance and recovery. While they don't contain as much potassium as avocados, they still have about 10 to 14 percent of the recommended daily value. Consuming potassium helps to avoid muscle cramps while exercising, so research suggests eating a banana before a workout. Additionally, since potassium is excreted through sweat, consuming bananas can help replete electrolytes to further boost workouts. However, eating bananas after a workout can also prove beneficial.

A 2018 study out of Appalachian State University, for example, found that a combination of water and a banana is likely more effective for exercise recovery than sports drinks.

### Nuts

Many types of nuts can be used in a variety of satiating snacks and meals, and many varieties strongly benefit muscle health. One serving of pistachios, for example, provides as much protein as one egg. Pistachios also have a higher ratio of essential amino acids than most other kinds of nuts. Additionally, peanuts are a prominent source of biotin, a vitamin that helps convert food into energy, which can help with overall workout performance and muscle building. For a low-carb, workout-friendly option, almonds contain just 2.5 grams of digestible carbs and only 161 calories in a small handful.

### Chickpeas

Whether tossed in a salad or blended into hummus, chickpeas are a versatile legume that can act as a meat replacement in any meal. They're also high in plant-based protein, with 14.5 grams per 1-cup cooked serving. The same serving contains 71 percent of the recommended daily value of folate, which helps convert carbohydrates into energy. Chickpeas contain nearly every essential amino acid that can be obtained from food, minus methionine. Pairing it with a grain that contains methionine, such as quinoa, can help you get a complete protein-based meal. ●

# MAXIMIZING MUSCLES

Keeping your body strong means more than just being able to do pull-ups or carry groceries with ease. From metabolism to hormonal health, here are some ways muscles matter.

**BY HALLIE LEVINE**

When we think about muscles, our minds quickly go to abs, quads, biceps and triceps—but of course we have hundreds more. "Muscles make up roughly 30 percent of a woman's body mass," says Naresh C. Rao, DO, a sports medicine physician in New York City. (For men, the percentage hovers at around 40 percent.) The more muscle you have, the more calories you burn.

And some good news: Despite what you may have heard, it's not inevitable that your muscles will wither as you age. There are simple and straightforward ways you can outsmart the clock and keep your metabolism cranked Here are three research-backed reasons you should focus on building strong muscles, plus advice that will help you get stronger all over.

## More Muscle Ups Your Metabolism

It's a cruel reality of weight loss: When people drop pounds, their metabolism often takes a dive. Fat cells make leptin, a chemical that tells your brain you're full. When leptin levels dip (which can happen if you're on a diet), your body slows its metabolism to conserve energy. But you can boost your burn by pumping iron. A 2015 study found that people who did resistance training for nine months had a roughly 5 percent increase in their resting metabolic rate. Getting more protein is key as well, says Caroline Apovian, MD, director of the Nutrition and Weight Management Center at Boston Medical Center. While the recommended dietary allowance is 0.8 grams per kilogram (0.36 grams per pound) of body weight per day, "my research shows that to prevent muscle loss while losing weight, you need to almost double that," she says.

DON'T RUSH! RESTING FOR A FEW MINUTES BETWEEN SETS MAY PROMOTE MUSCLE GROWTH.

## Menopause Isn't Kind to Muscles

Estrogen appears to be related to muscle strength, which means that as your estrogen levels decline, your muscles may get weaker. One thing that might help: a vitamin D supplement. A 2015 study published in the journal *Osteoporosis International* found that postmenopausal women who took 1,000 IU of $D_3$ per day for nine months had a 25 percent increase in their muscle strength; the women taking a placebo had a 7 percent drop in muscle mass. But popping a pill isn't enough to fight the decline, stresses JoAnn Pinkerton, MD, executive director of the North American Menopause Society and professor of obstetrics and gynecology at the University of Virginia Health System. "Strength training is also needed," she says—ideally, you should do two or three workouts a week.

## Inflammation May Help Heal Muscles

After a gym session, you may be tempted to pop an over-the-counter anti-inflammatory to ward off soreness. But post-workout inflammation—which is temporary, as opposed to chronic inflammation—might be a good thing. Researchers from Brigham Young University found that after exercise, pro-inflammatory T cells infiltrate damaged muscle fibers, possibly to help repair the tissue; after a repeat round of exercise, inflammation increases. "One of our theories is that this inflammation is a healthy process your body uses to heal muscles," says senior author Robert Hyldahl, PhD, associate professor of exercise sciences. What's more, "inflammation and post-exercise soreness didn't actually seem to be linked." In fact, folks experienced less soreness after their second round of exercise, when inflammation was higher. Try easing aches with ice or moist heat instead of meds. ●

# THE TRUTH ABOUT PROTEIN

We need more. We need less. Beef is best. Beans are better. Fed up with your friends' conflicting Facebook posts? Here's how you can power up your plate for real.

**BY AVIVA PATZ**

Protein is crucial to nearly every bodily function. We need it to have energy, to feel full, to build and repair muscle, to process nutrients and boost immunity, to send chemical signals—basically, to stay alive. And with so much new research pointing to the nutrient's power as a hunger buster and super sculptor, it's easy to think the more protein, the better. "Many women I see are making a conscious effort to get more protein in their diet," says Rachel Begun, RDN, a dietitian and culinary nutritionist in Los Angeles. But is that wise? Ahead, the most evolved advice.

## How Much Do You Really Need?

The recommended dietary allowance (RDA), which is the minimum amount you need to be healthy, is 0.8 grams per kilogram (0.36 grams per pound)

MAKING AN EFFORT TO SWAP MEAT FOR PLANT-BASED PROTEINS CAN HELP LOWER YOUR RISK OF SOME DISEASES.

of body weight per day—46 grams for an average woman. That equals as little as 10 percent of your daily calories. If you're not super active, that's likely adequate, and you'll hit the target effortlessly if you follow a typical Western diet. In fact, American women already eat about 68 grams of protein a day, according to the latest data from the National Health and Nutrition Examination Survey. "There's no reason to go out of your way to get protein," says Dariush Mozaffarian, MD, dean of the Tufts Friedman School of Nutrition Science & Policy. "Just eat a variety of fish, nuts, beans, seeds and dairy, including yogurt."

However, increasing your protein well above the RDA may make sense if...

**YOU'RE VERY ACTIVE.** That means you get at least 35 to 40 minutes of moderate exercise four or five days a week, including resistance training two or more times a week. Consider eating 1.2 to 2 grams of dietary protein per kilogram (or about 0.5 to 0.9 grams per pound) of your body weight each day, says Nancy Rodriguez, PhD, professor of nutritional sciences at the University of Connecticut. That amount is best for rebuilding muscle tissue, especially if you do a lot of high-intensity workouts, research suggests.

**YOU'RE TRYING TO LOSE WEIGHT.** Protein takes longer to digest than carbs, helping you feel full, and it also pushes your body to secrete the gut hormone peptide YY, which reduces hunger. "When you bring protein to about 30 percent of your daily calories, you'll naturally eat less," says Lauren Slayton, RD, founder of Foodtrainers, a nutrition practice in New York City, and author of *The Little Book of Thin*. "Protein decreases appetite and also, in my experience, helps you manage cravings."

While research is mixed about whether consuming more protein leads to weight loss, it's pretty clear that protein can help you retain more lean muscle as you lose fat. One 2011 study suggests amping up protein to as much as 1.8 to 2 grams per kilogram (roughly 0.8 to 0.9 grams per pound) of body weight per day to stave off muscle loss when restricting calories. Cut back on refined carbs to balance out the extra calories from adding protein.

**YOU'RE IN MIDDLE AGE.** Eating more protein as you get older may help you maintain muscle and ward off osteoporosis, "so you can stay stronger and more functional," says Rodriguez. In a 2015 study, adults over the age of 50 who roughly doubled the RDA (eating 1.5 grams of protein per kilogram, or 0.68 grams per pound, of body weight per day) were better able to rebuild and retain muscle after only four days, compared with control groups eating the RDA.

Doubling the RDA gives you "optimal protein," a concept that Rodriguez and more than 40 nutrition scientists advanced at a recent Protein Summit, the findings from which were published in 2015 in the *American Journal of Clinical Nutrition*. Optimal protein works out to be about 15 to 25 percent of your daily calories, still below the level recommended by many popular high-protein diets. Over a day, that could look like 20 to 30 grams per meal and 12 to 15 grams per snack, for a total of 90 to 105 grams daily.

## The Dangers of Loading Up

When experts decry protein-heavy diets, the issue is usually not quantity but quality. "It's not protein per se that's a problem, but the 'passengers' it brings with it," explains Tom Rifai, MD, regional medical

### 10 REAL-FOOD BOOSTS

Powders have their place (assuming you're picking one with superclean ingredients), but they're not the only way to amp up your intake. Try these easy hacks to add whole-food protein to a meal or snack.

**1.** Prepare ½ cup oatmeal with 1 cup milk (8g) instead of water.

**2.** Sprinkle 2 tablespoons chia seeds (6g) onto 2 slices avocado toast.

**3.** Blend ½ cup silken tofu (6g) into soup or a smoothie.

**4.** Toss ¼ cup cashews (5g) into a stir-fry.

**5.** Blend 3 tablespoons hemp seeds (9g) into salad dressing (try one made with olive oil, lemon juice, garlic, and herbs).

**6.** Add 2 tablespoons pumpkin seeds (5g) to granola.

**7.** Scatter 1 cup green peas (8g) over pasta.

**8.** Top pancakes or waffles with 2 tablespoons almond butter (7g) instead of maple syrup.

**9.** Add ½ cup canned black beans (7g), drained and rinsed, to salsa.

**10.** Trade cream cheese for ¼ cup cottage cheese (6g) on a toasted bagel.

director of metabolic health and weight management for the Henry Ford Health System in Detroit. "You can't compare egg whites, fish or beans to fatty porterhouse steak." Eating a lot of meat means getting a ton of calories and saturated fat as well as a digestive by-product called TMAO, all of which can contribute to higher risks of certain cancers, diabetes and cardiovascular disease. Indeed, a 2014 study published in *Cell Metabolism* showed a hike in cancer mortality risk for people who ate more animal protein in midlife. On the flip side, a new study from the Harvard T.H. Chan School of Public Health found that adults who ate a plant-based diet and dropped one or two servings of animal-based foods (to four or fewer servings a day) cut their risk of type 2 diabetes by up to 20 percent. The takeaway: If you want to bump up your protein, grab those extra grams from plant sources or even fish (both of which offer additional beneficial nutrients on top of protein) rather than red meat.

### Eat Early, Eat Often

Folks who ate 35 grams of protein at breakfast consumed 400 fewer calories throughout the day and lost more body fat than those who ate a breakfast with 13 grams or skipped an a.m. meal entirely, according to a 2015 study from the University of Missouri. "I've seen many women who, after shifting more of their daily protein to breakfast and lunch, stay more satiated, preventing overeating in the late afternoon and evening," says Begun. A sample high-protein breakfast: 6 ounces of nonfat Greek yogurt (17 grams of protein) with 1/4 cup of almonds (8 grams), 2 tablespoons of sunflower seeds (4 grams) and 1/2 cup of mixed berries (1 gram).

More incentive to add protein earlier in the day: Other research suggests that it does the best job of keeping your muscles in rebuilding mode if you spread your intake over the day's meals and snacks rather than cramming in most of it at dinner. Eating all your protein at one sitting also backfires because your system can process only so much at once—about 25 to 40 grams, for most people. "If you can't use the extra protein, your body just turns it into carbs," explains Dr. Rifai.

### Go Complete

"Complete protein" is a term often used for foods that contain, in the right proportion for our dietary needs, all nine of the essential amino acids our bodies can't manufacture themselves. (We can make the 11 other amino acids from scratch.) Think of your amino acid requirements like a Scrabble game: "Some letters you need over and over again, like E, and some you don't need as many of, like Z," says Christopher Gardner, PhD, professor of medicine and director of nutrition studies at the Stanford Prevention Research Center. Animal products, such as chicken, fish and eggs, provide the right letters (amino acids) in close to the right proportion that we need to spell words (build proteins in the body). Certain plant-based foods (quinoa, soybeans, amaranth, buckwheat) also provide roughly the proper proportion of amino acids.

Other plants contain all the essential amino acids, but not in the optimal proportion—usually there's not enough of one or more of them, which is why the classic advice for vegetarians and vegans has been to pair complementary foods, like rice and beans, in order to make a complete protein. The good news is, it doesn't need to be that complicated. As long as your weekly diet includes a reasonable variety and amount of beans, whole grains, nuts and seeds (for example, lentils, chickpeas, oats, brown rice, walnuts, almonds and sunflower seeds), it's likely that you're getting what you need.

### Workout Wisdom

"Ideally, you should get 20 grams of protein within 30 to 40 minutes post-workout for optimal muscle recovery and growth," says sports dietitian Marjorie Cohn, RDN. That said, you can't chug a protein shake after spin class and skimp on protein the rest of the time. You still need a healthy total amount spread out through your day. ●

## POWER TRIP

Here are the steps protein takes in your body, from first bite to final exit.

**STEP 1:** You eat some grilled chicken or a plate of beans.

**STEP 2:** Stomach acids and gut enzymes break down the proteins in the chicken or beans into amino acids, the building blocks of protein.

**STEP 3:** Amino acids are absorbed through the walls of your small intestine and enter the bloodstream. In addition to helping build muscle, these amino acids help produce, maintain and repair numerous proteins throughout your body, including antibodies, hormones and neurotransmitters.

**STEP 4:** Extra amino acids aren't stored for much longer than 24 hours (that's why you have to eat protein every day), so once the body has used what it needs, the leftovers go to the liver. There, some are converted into glucose and used as a fuel source. Nitrogen by-products from amino acid breakdown are excreted in urine.

+

YOU COULD MEET THE DAILY MINIMUM DIETARY GUIDELINES FOR WOMEN WITH A 5- TO 6-OUNCE PIECE OF CHICKEN.

# DOES MILK REALLY DO A BODY GOOD?

This calcium superstar's bone-health benefits have been called into question. Here's what you need to know.

**BY HOLLY PEVZNER**

Milk has been billed as a mighty bone-bolsterer since well before the days of the celebrity milk mustache. Bones are made up mostly of calcium, and research shows that getting plenty of this nutrient early in life builds bone mass. "So of course you'd think, keep eating calcium as an adult for strong bones—and in turn, prevent fractures," says Walter Willett, MD, a professor of epidemiology and nutrition at Harvard T.H. Chan School of Public Health in Boston.

However, recent research has turned this conventional wisdom on its head—at least when it comes to adults—and caused a lot of public confusion. A study published in the *British Medical Journal* found that every serving of milk increased the risk of a bone fracture by 9 percent. And a 2017 meta-analysis in the *Journal of the American Medical Association* concluded that calcium supplements did nothing to reduce the risk of breaking a bone. What gives?

First, the *BMJ* study showed only that people who drank more milk had more fractures. What it *didn't* prove? That the dairy product, rather than some other factor, caused those fractures. Even the researchers say that women who have osteoporosis—which means they already have an increased risk of fractures—may be seeking out more milk for its bone health reputation, not that the milk itself weakened their bones.

If drinking milk doesn't cause fractures, will it help prevent them? "That's a little complicated," says Shivani Sahni, PhD, director of nutrition at the Hinda and Arthur Marcus Institute for Aging Research in Boston, who studies diet and osteoporosis. "The calcium you get from dairy is essential

+
IF YOU'RE AVOIDING MILK BECAUSE OF DIETARY RESTRICTIONS, CONSIDER ALTERNATIVE CALCIUM SOURCES.

KALE HAS AROUND 250MG OF CALCIUM PER 100G, HIGHER THAN WHOLE MILK'S 110MG PER 100G.

for building bone mass through your early 20s. It also helps prevent bone loss later in life. But the association between dairy consumption and a lower risk of fracture isn't well established. There haven't been enough studies." And some studies show it can reduce breaks, while others say it can't. The research has been just as inconclusive about calcium supplements. In 2018, the U.S. Preventive Services Task Force, an independent panel of experts, reviewed all the data and concluded that there's not enough evidence to recommend women take calcium supplements to stave off bone breaks.

So how can calcium help prevent bone loss but possibly have no influence on fracture risk? Again: It's complicated. Your personal risk of breaks involves a lot more than just one mineral. "Hormonal changes after menopause, low physical activity, low muscle mass, balance issues—all of these factors greatly influence your odds of fracture," says Dr. Willett. Also, Sahni says, think about it like this: If you have osteoporosis, your goal is fracture prevention. If you don't, then you want to prevent osteoporosis—and to do that you should, among other things, consume calcium.

The USDA recommends that most adults get 1,000 milligrams of the mineral a day. Aside from dairy, good sources include soybeans, salmon and leafy greens. The bulk of your calcium should be coming from your diet, says Sahni, because when you focus on food, you garner other benefits. "Lean protein, vitamin C, carotenoids, magnesium and other nutrients are all needed for bone health," she says. A study published in the *European Journal of Nutrition* found that people following a Mediterranean-style diet, filled with produce, nuts, fish and whole grains, had a 21 percent lower risk of hip fracture than those who ate a lot of sugar, refined grains and red meat. So consume a variety of calcium-rich foods. If you want to talk to your doctor about a supplement, that's fine—just think of it as a safety net, not a primary calcium source. Also, make vitamin D a priority—it helps your body absorb calcium.

Although calcium gets much of the attention when it comes to bone health, it's far from the only solution. Regular exercise may be even more important, and there's no controversy there. "The proof is amazingly consistent: Physical activity, like resistance training and weight-bearing exercise, is very good for preventing fractures," says Dr. Willett. "It's probably the most important thing you can do to keep your bones healthy." ●

# HEALTHY DINNER RECIPES

If you're trying to build muscle or lose weight, protein is a key nutrient—especially at dinner. Here are seven days' worth of easy meals to add to your weeknight menu.

## Chili-Topped Sweet Potatoes

**ACTIVE**: 30 minutes
**TOTAL**: 30 minutes

*Transform ordinary baked sweet potatoes into a full dinner with this chili-topped version. Sprinkle on extra toppings as you see fit—sliced scallions, chopped fresh cilantro, diced avocado and sliced jalapeños are all tasty choices. To make ahead: Refrigerate chili (step 1) for up to three days, or freeze for up to three months.*

- 1 pound lean ground beef
- ¾ cup finely chopped white onion
- ½ cup finely chopped red bell pepper
- 4 cloves garlic, chopped
- 2 tablespoons chili powder
- 1 tablespoon ground cumin
- 2 teaspoons dried oregano
- 1 teaspoon ground coriander
- 1 14-ounce can diced tomatoes
- ¼ cup water
- 4 medium sweet potatoes
- ½ cup shredded cheese, such as Cheddar or pepper Jack

**1.** Cook beef, onion, bell pepper and garlic in a large skillet over medium-high heat, crumbling the beef with a spatula, until the meat is browned, 8 to 10 minutes. Stir in chili powder, cumin, oregano and coriander; cook, stirring, for 30 seconds. Add tomatoes (with their juice) and water and simmer for 5 minutes.
**2.** Meanwhile, prick sweet potatoes with a fork in several places. Microwave on high until tender all the way through, 12 to 15 minutes.
**3.** Serve the sweet potatoes topped with the chili and cheese.

**SERVES 4:** 1 CUP CHILI & 1 SWEET POTATO EACH
**CAL** 418, **FAT** 18G (SAT 7G), **CHOL** 88MG, **CARBS** 35G, **TOTAL SUGARS** 12G (ADDED 0G), **PROTEIN** 31G, **FIBER** 9G, **SODIUM** 451MG, **POTASSIUM** 1,300MG.

+
TRY CANNED BLACK BEANS INSTEAD OF GROUND BEEF FOR A VEGETARIAN SWAP.

## Grilled Flank Steak with Tomato Salad

**ACTIVE:** 10 minutes
**TOTAL:** 20 minutes

*Cutting the steak immediately after cooking breaks all the rules of meat cookery, but in this recipe we do it intentionally in order to capture the juices and incorporate them into the dressing. Serve with crusty bread to soak up the deliciousness.*

- **1 pint grape tomatoes, halved**
- **½ cup chopped fresh cilantro**
- **⅓ cup extra-virgin olive oil**
- **1 small jalapeño pepper, seeded and sliced**
- **2 teaspoons finely chopped garlic**
- **½ teaspoon salt, divided**
- **1 1-pound flank steak**
- **½ teaspoon ground pepper**

**1.** Preheat grill to medium-high or heat a grill pan over medium-high heat.
**2.** Combine tomatoes, cilantro, oil, jalapeño, garlic and ¼ teaspoon salt in a medium bowl; set aside.
**3.** Season steak with the remaining ¼ teaspoon salt and pepper. Grill until an instant-read thermometer inserted in the center reads 125°F for medium-rare, 3 to 5 minutes per side.
**4.** Transfer the steak to a clean cutting board, preferably one with grooves for collecting juices, and thinly slice across the grain. Divide the slices among four plates. Drizzle any juices that have accumulated on the cutting board over the steak, and top with the tomato salad.

**SERVES 4:** 3 OZ. STEAK & ½ CUP SALAD EACH
**CAL** 346, **FAT** 25G (SAT 5G), **CHOL** 70MG, **CARBS** 4G, **TOTAL SUGARS** 2G (ADDED 0G), **PROTEIN** 25G, **FIBER** 1G, **SODIUM** 358MG, **POTASSIUM** 591MG.

## Greek Salad with Edamame

**ACTIVE**: 30 minutes
**TOTAL**: 30 minutes

*Edamame adds vegetarian protein and vibrant color to the classic Greek salad. Serve with toasted pita brushed with olive oil and sprinkled with dried oregano or za'atar.*

- ¼ cup red-wine vinegar
- 3 tablespoons extra-virgin olive oil
- ¼ teaspoon salt
- ¼ teaspoon ground pepper
- 8 cups chopped romaine (about 2 romaine hearts)
- 16 ounces frozen shelled edamame (about 3 cups), thawed
- 1 cup halved cherry or grape tomatoes
- ½ European cucumber, sliced
- ½ cup crumbled feta cheese
- ¼ cup slivered fresh basil
- ¼ cup sliced Kalamata olives
- ¼ cup slivered red onion

Whisk vinegar, oil, salt and pepper in a large bowl. Add romaine, edamame, tomatoes, cucumber, feta, basil, olives and onion; toss.

**SERVES 4:** 2¾ CUPS EACH
**CAL** 344, **FAT** 23G (SAT 5G), **CHOL** 17MG, **CARBS** 20G, **TOTAL SUGARS** 6G (ADDED 0G), **PROTEIN** 17G, **FIBER** 9G, **SODIUM** 489MG, **POTASSIUM** 908MG.

## Cauliflower Chicken Fried "Rice"

**ACTIVE**: 35 minutes
**TOTAL**: 35 minutes

*Get an extra serving of vegetables and cut back on carbs by replacing rice with riced cauliflower in this healthy chicken fried rice recipe.*

- 1 teaspoon peanut oil plus 2 tablespoons, divided
- 2 large eggs, beaten
- 3 scallions, thinly sliced, whites and greens separated
- 1 tablespoon grated fresh ginger
- 1 tablespoon minced garlic
- 1 pound boneless, skinless chicken thighs, trimmed and cut into ½-inch pieces
- ½ cup diced red bell pepper
- 1 cup snow peas, trimmed and halved
- 4 cups cauliflower rice
- 3 tablespoons reduced-sodium tamari or soy sauce
- 1 teaspoon sesame oil (optional)

**1.** Heat 1 teaspoon oil in a large flat-bottomed carbon-steel wok or large heavy skillet over high heat. Add eggs and cook, without stirring, until fully cooked on one side, about 30 seconds. Flip and cook until just cooked through, about 15 seconds. Transfer to a cutting board and cut into ½-inch pieces.

**2.** Add 1 tablespoon oil to the pan along with scallion whites, ginger and garlic; cook, stirring, until the scallions have softened, about 30 seconds. Add chicken and cook, stirring, for 1 minute. Add bell pepper and snow peas; cook, stirring, until just tender, 2 to 4 minutes. Transfer everything to a large plate.

**3.** Add the remaining 1 tablespoon oil to the pan; add cauliflower rice and stir until beginning to soften, about 2 minutes.

**4.** Return the chicken mixture and eggs to the pan; add tamari or soy sauce and sesame oil (if using) and stir until well combined. Garnish with scallion greens.

**SERVES 4:** 1¼ CUPS EACH
**CAL** 304, **FAT** 15G (SAT 4G, MONO 6G), **CHOL** 200MG, **CARBS** 12G, **TOTAL SUGARS** 5G (ADDED 0G), **PROTEIN** 30G, **FIBER** 4G, **SODIUM** 591MG, **POTASSIUM** 883MG.

## Chicken Cutlets with Sun-Dried Tomato Cream Sauce

**ACTIVE**: 20 minutes
**TOTAL**: 20 minutes

*A jar of sun-dried tomatoes does double duty here: The flavorful oil they're packed in is used to sauté the chicken, and the tomatoes go into the cream sauce.*

- **1 pound chicken cutlets**
- **¼ teaspoon salt, divided**
- **¼ teaspoon ground pepper, divided**
- **½ cup slivered oil-packed sun-dried tomatoes, plus 1 tablespoon oil from the jar**
- **½ cup finely chopped shallots**
- **½ cup dry white wine**
- **½ cup heavy cream**
- **2 tablespoons chopped fresh parsley**

**1.** Sprinkle chicken with ⅛ teaspoon each salt and pepper. Heat sun-dried tomato oil in a large skillet over medium heat. Add the chicken and cook, turning once, until browned and an instant-read thermometer inserted into the thickest part registers 165°F, about 6 minutes total. Transfer to a plate.

**2.** Add sun-dried tomatoes and shallots to the pan. Cook, stirring, for 1 minute. Increase heat to high and add wine. Cook, scraping up any browned bits, until the liquid has mostly evaporated, about 2 minutes. Reduce heat to medium and stir in cream, any accumulated juices from the chicken and the remaining ⅛ teaspoon each salt and pepper; simmer for 2 minutes. Return the chicken to the pan and turn to coat with the sauce. Serve the chicken topped with the sauce and parsley.

**SERVES 4:** 3 OZ. CHICKEN & ¼ CUP SAUCE EACH

**CAL** 324, **FAT** 19G (SAT 8G), **CHOL** 97MG, **CARBS** 8G, **TOTAL SUGARS** 2G (ADDED 0G), **PROTEIN** 25G, **FIBER** 1G, **SODIUM** 250MG, **POTASSIUM** 532MG.

## Chicken Hummus Bowls

**ACTIVE**: 25 minutes
**TOTAL**: 25 minutes

*The spiced chicken atop these bowls is ready fast with the help of the broiler. Serve with warm whole-wheat pita for scooping up extra hummus at the bottom of the bowl.*

- **1 pound boneless, skinless chicken thighs, trimmed and cut into 1-inch pieces**
- **3 tablespoons extra-virgin olive oil, divided**
- **1 teaspoon ground cumin**
- **1 teaspoon paprika**
- **¼ teaspoon cayenne pepper**
- **¼ teaspoon salt, divided**
- **2 cloves garlic, finely chopped**
- **2 tablespoons lemon juice**
- **2 cups hummus**
- **1 English cucumber, halved lengthwise and sliced**
- **1 pint cherry tomatoes, halved**
- **¼ cup slivered red onion**
- **¼ cup chopped fresh parsley**

**1.** Position rack in upper third of oven; preheat broiler to high. Line a rimmed baking sheet with foil.
**2.** Toss chicken with 1 tablespoon oil, cumin, paprika, cayenne and ⅛ teaspoon salt. Spread evenly on the prepared pan. Broil until just cooked through, 5 to 7 minutes.
**3.** Meanwhile, mash garlic and the remaining ⅛ teaspoon salt into a paste with a fork. Transfer to a medium bowl and whisk in lemon juice and the remaining 2 tablespoons oil. Add the chicken and let stand for 5 minutes, stirring occasionally.
**4.** Divide hummus among 4 shallow bowls or plates. Top with the chicken and any remaining dressing, cucumber, tomatoes, onion and parsley. Serve with warm whole-wheat pita.

**SERVES 4:** ½ CUP EACH HUMMUS, CHICKEN, TOMATOES & CUCUMBER
**CAL** 485, **FAT** 29G (SAT 5G), **CHOL** 104MG, **CARBS** 27G, **TOTAL SUGARS** 4G (ADDED 0G), **PROTEIN** 31G, **FIBER** 10G, **SODIUM** 712MG, **POTASSIUM** 886MG.

## Vegan Meatballs

**ACTIVE**: 40 minutes
**TOTAL**: 1 hour 10 minutes

*For these hearty and healthy vegan meatballs, we've swapped out the traditional ground beef and pork for protein-packed chickpeas and quinoa—without skimping on any of those Italian flavors you look for in a classic meatball. Mushrooms up the umami factor, and simple tomato sauce completes the picture. Serve over your favorite pasta or enjoy on their own. To make ahead: Prepare meatballs (Steps 1–4) and refrigerate up to 1 day. Prepare sauce (Step 4) and refrigerate up to 3 days.*

- **2½ cups small cauliflower florets**
- **8 ounces white mushrooms, halved**
- **½ small onion, coarsely chopped**
- **2 large cloves garlic, divided**
- **4 tablespoons extra-virgin olive oil, divided**
- **1½ teaspoons Italian seasoning, divided**
- **½ teaspoon salt, divided**
- **¼ teaspoon ground pepper**
- **1 tablespoon tomato paste**
- **1 cup canned chickpeas**
- **2 cups cooked quinoa**
- **1 tablespoon reduced-sodium tamari or soy sauce**
- **1 28-ounce can no-salt-added crushed tomatoes**
- **½ teaspoon crushed red pepper**
- **2 tablespoons chopped fresh basil**

**1.** Preheat oven to 400°F. Coat a large rimmed baking sheet with cooking spray.

**2.** Pulse cauliflower, mushrooms, onion and 1 garlic clove in a food processor until finely chopped, about 15 pulses. Heat 2 tablespoons oil in a large skillet over medium-high heat. Add the cauliflower mixture, ¾ teaspoon Italian seasoning and ¼ teaspoon each salt and pepper; cook, stirring, until softened, about 5 minutes. Add tomato paste and cook, stirring, for 1 minute more. Transfer to a large bowl and let cool, stirring a few times, for 5 minutes.

**3.** Add chickpeas to the food processor; puree until smooth. Add the chickpea mixture to the large bowl along with quinoa and tamari or soy sauce; stir to combine. Form the mixture into 24 balls (about 2½ tablespoons each) and place on the prepared baking sheet.

**4.** Bake the meatballs until heated through and firm, 20 to 25 minutes. Let cool on the baking sheet for 3 minutes.

**5.** Meanwhile, finely chop the remaining garlic clove. Heat the remaining 2 tablespoons oil in a large skillet over medium heat. Add the garlic, tomatoes, crushed red pepper and the remaining ¾ teaspoon Italian seasoning and ¼ teaspoon salt. Bring to a simmer. Cook until the flavors have melded, about 5 minutes. Serve the meatballs with the sauce, sprinkled with basil.

**SERVES 6:** 4 MEATBALLS & ½ CUP SAUCE EACH

**CAL** 394, **FAT** 17G (SAT 2G), **CHOL** 0MG, **CARBS** 46G, **TOTAL SUGARS** 12G (ADDED 0G), **PROTEIN** 13G, **FIBER** 10G, **SODIUM** 434MG, **POTASSIUM** 1,272MG.

CHAPTER 2

# GETTING STRONGER

These beginner-friendly workouts, as well as some crucial fitness advice, can put your body on its healthiest path.

+

MOVE FASTER BETWEEN SETS TO TORCH EXTRA CALORIES DURING STRENGTH TRAINING.

# WHY STRENGTH TRAINING IS A WEIGHT-LOSS WINNER

Don't spend all your energy on the treadmill if you're trying to drop a pants size. Strength training is an important way to boost your weight loss. Here's why—and how.

**BY LAURIE HERR**

Trying to lose a few pounds, but the scale won't budge? Try adding more weight at the gym. Weight training—using free weights or weight machines to build muscle—is a type of strength training that not can only help you slim down but also offers a ton of other health benefits.

The best part: You don't have to spend all your time in the weight room. You can even do it at home, without any fancy equipment. Here's why weight training may be what you need to get the scale moving in the right direction, plus a few tips and exercises to get you started.

## Burn More Calories

It's really pretty simple: Weight training builds muscle, and muscle burns more calories than fat—up to three times more, according to some estimates.

"Muscles are fat-burning machines," says Wendy Batts, a regional master instructor for the National Academy of Sports Medicine. "So the more muscle you have, the more calories you're going to burn."

It doesn't end after you leave the gym, either. Your body keeps torching calories for the next 24 to 48 hours as it works to repair stressed muscle tissues. That's known as the afterburn effect, another name for excess post-exercise oxygen consumption (EPOC). The more oxygen you use both during and after a workout, the greater the EPOC. And studies show that strength training is one of the best ways to do it.

All of this is very good news if you're trying to lose weight.

Think about it. With weight training, you're revving up your calorie burn. You're boosting your metabolism—possibly by up to 5 percent, according to one nine-month study. And since you're likely already watching what you eat, your exercise routine is now working with your diet to help you shed unwanted pounds.

"Obviously, burning more calories throughout your day, combined with a sensible diet, is going to maximize your weight loss," Batts says. Not only that, but it helps keep the weight off. One study found that less than an hour and a half of resistance training each week helped keep dieters from gaining back weight, especially harmful belly fat.

**Bodyweight exercises such as planks or pull-ups require zero equipment and are super effective for getting stronger, leaner, and fitter.**

## The Health Benefits of Strength Training

The benefits go beyond the bathroom scale, too. "Weight training improves your posture, helps your endurance, builds strength and reduces your chance of injuries," Batts says. Research shows it can also boost heart health, improve cholesterol levels and increase bone density. It also slows the inevitable decline in strength as we age, because it keeps our muscles from turning to mush and being replaced with fat as we get older.

Oh, and something weight training doesn't do: It won't make you bulk up. "If you're training to be a body builder, you're going to be eating more. You're going to be training with heavy weights, doing fewer reps and isolating different muscles," Batts explains. "To lose weight, you're going to monitor your calorie intake and do more reps with lighter weights." The end result: a leaner, stronger, more toned body. Who doesn't want that?

## Getting Started

"Where people get into trouble is when they start by lifting too heavy," Batts says. "They go to the gym, pick up 10 pounds and then try to lunge or squat or curl. And the next day they're so sore and miserable that they get discouraged and quit."

Instead, she suggests starting with your own body weight (read on for some suggested moves). Your goal is to do 12 to 15 repetitions—they should feel like a challenge, but you should still be able to keep your form. As you get stronger, you'll gradually add more weight.

No dumbbells at home? Household items will do. Start with soup cans and slowly work up to lifting milk or laundry detergent jugs (partially filled). Try carrying a full laundry basket while you do a set of walking lunges. "You don't have to have a really heavy weight in the beginning, especially if it's for weight loss," Batts says.

Finally, remember to change things up. "Do something new every week—even if it's just a little change—so you're challenging your body in a different way," Batts says. "You'll be using different muscles and expending more calories." If you always do cardio first, switch the order and start with weights instead. One study suggests weight training first gets your heart rate up, making your cardio workout more efficient.

## Weight-Training Exercises to Try

Try the strength-building moves below. Be sure to warm up first. Watch your form, and keep a slow tempo. If you feel pain, stop.

**FLOOR BRIDGE** Lie face-up on the floor, with knees bent and feet flat on the ground. Keep arms at your sides with palms down. Lift hips off the ground, squeezing your glutes and core until your knees, hips and shoulders form a straight line. Hold for three seconds at the top, then lower back down to starting position.

**HIP THRUST** Start in a seated position with your knees and feet flat on the floor and your shoulder blades (not your neck!) against a bench. Add weight to your hip crease using a pad, if needed. Squeeze your glutes and core and lift your hips until your back is parallel to the floor.

**BODYWEIGHT SQUAT** Stand with your feet slightly wider than hip-width apart, toes slightly turned out, arms at your sides, palms in. Squeeze your core and keep your chest lifted and back flat as you shift your weight into your heels, push your hips back, and bend your knees to lower into a squat. Bend your elbows and bring your palms together in front of your chest. (You can also just hold your hands in front of your chest the entire time.) Push through your heels to stand back up, and squeeze your glutes at the top for one rep. ●

# 5 Power Foods to Fuel Your Workout

## Want a better sweat session? Find out which fitness foods can help improve your workout.

**BY JOYCE HENDLEY**

Want to give your routine a boost? Five key ingredients can give your body an extra edge when exercising or recovering from your workout. Here are the ingredients that can help power your next exercise session.

**1. PEANUTS**

The most protein-rich nut of them all gives you quality protein, which is important for muscle building.

**Pre-workout:** A little protein staves off hunger without overtaxing digestion.

**Post-workout:** Protein helps repair muscles and stokes your body's muscle-building machinery, especially when consumed within a half hour after exercise.

**2. OATS**

Oats are rich in carbohydrates, the fuel your muscles prefer.

**Pre-workout:** Fiber-rich oats supply sustained energy.

**Post-workout:** They provide a healthy amount of carbs to replenish depleted glycogen stores.

**3. DRIED BLUEBERRIES**

Dried blueberries are a super tasty and antioxidant-rich alternative to raisins.

**Pre-workout:** The easily digested carbohydrates in blueberries fuel muscles, and their fiber provides staying power.

**Post-workout:** Polyphenolic compounds in blueberries may help combat oxidative stress in muscles, potentially preventing soreness and inflammation.

**4. CHOCOLATE CHIPS**

You probably don't need us to justify why you should snack on a handful of chocolate chips or an energy bar containing them, but there actually are some great health reasons for adding them.

**Pre-workout:** Antioxidants in dark chocolate help prevent muscle soreness later on. One study of cyclists showed that dark chocolate helped reduce oxidative stress in muscles, a component of soreness. Animal research suggests chocolate's epicatechins can boost leg strength and endurance capacity.

**Post-workout:** Dark chocolate provides flavonols, compounds that can help improve blood flow, which brings more oxygen to replenish your hardworking muscles.

**5. PUMPKIN SEEDS**

Pumpkin seeds are good sources of alpha-linolenic acid, a plant form of omega-3 fatty acids that can help fight inflammation, a factor in muscle soreness. While they're not as potent as fish-based omega-3s in producing these benefits, they're also (like exercise) good for your heart.

**Pre-workout:** Snack on some pumpkin seeds a few hours before your workout to bolster your energy.

**Post-workout:** Pumpkin seeds are a good source of zinc, a key nutrient for recovery that helps repair muscle tissue.

# Walk This Way

## Hoofing it with poles might seem a little weird, but get this: Nordic walking gives you cardio plus a full-body strength workout. Talk about effective!

**BY KAREN ASP**

Ever since I started Nordic walking on the paved trails where I live in Indiana, I've drawn a lot of attention to myself. People comment on the poles I use, shouting out things like "Where's the snow?" or "Are you asphalt skiing?" I honestly don't mind. It's a chance for me to rave about the health benefits of the sport. And little do they know: I've competed in Nordic walking for almost a decade, snagging six world championships and six world records. (Two still stand.)

The quirky-looking activity is common in parts of Europe, where it started as a method of dry-land training for cross-country skiers and then became a favorite mainstream form of exercise. As with cross-country skiing, you use specially designed poles to propel yourself forward. Nordic walking poles are shorter than ski poles, with secure hand straps and angled rubber feet to help you push against the ground, lengthening your stride so you can go faster and engaging the muscles in your core, chest, shoulders and arms. In fact, this full-body workout burns 20 to 46 percent more calories than regular walking, says Malin Svensson, author of *Nordic Walking.* And by distributing the workload more evenly throughout your body, you won't feel like you're putting in any more effort—although your heart rate may say otherwise. Even better: A systematic review published in the *American Journal of Preventive Medicine* found that Nordic walking was more effective than brisk walking at lowering resting heart rate and blood pressure, and boosting aerobic capacity. Some studies in the review also found that Nordic walking raised heart rate and oxygen consumption levels as much as jogging did—but in a joint-friendly way. And a study by researchers at Stanford and the University of Florida showed that walking with poles reduced stress at the knee joint by about 30 percent compared with strolling without them.

Nordic walking has a technique all its own, so there is a small learning curve. You can find great Nordic walking tutorials on YouTube, but you essentially start by strapping on the poles (I recommend Leki's Instructor Lite, $150 a pair, leki.mwrc.net) and dragging them alongside you as you walk normally while keeping your back straight. Once that feels natural, you can start pushing the poles into the ground and swinging your arms even more, thinking about reaching your arm forward as if you were about to shake somebody's hand, and then allowing your grip to relax as you propel your arm behind your hip as you move.

Take the poles out for a spin once, and who knows? Maybe you'll follow in my footsteps and fall so hard for this sport that you set a new record—even if it's just in your own neighborhood. ●

YOU CAN ACTIVATE
90 PERCENT
OF YOUR MUSCLES
WITH NORDIC
WALKING!

# The 6 Best At-Home Exercises

## We spoke with Julie Jones, wellness expert and personal trainer, about the best bodyweight exercises you can do at home.

**BY LAUREN WICKS**

Whether you don't have time to go to the gym or just prefer working out at home, it's great to keep a few bodyweight moves in your back pocket. We spoke with Julie Jones, CPT, a personal trainer and corporate wellness manager based in Atlanta, to find out her favorite exercises for a full-body workout in the comfort of your own space.

"Taking some time to get away from our screens and the news is good for our mental health," she says. "There are a ton of ways to remain active at home and help you do what makes your body feel good."

Jones says a good full-body workout should incorporate upper-body, lower-body, and core exercises, plus cardio. The following moves require no equipment, but you could easily add weight to any of them (a pair of five-pound weights is a great place to start). She advises doing these moves in timed increments instead of performing a certain number of reps, which will challenge and help you set realistic goals.

**SQUATS**

"Squats are a foundational movement in exercise because they are functional for life," Jones says. "We need to be able to bend down and lift things, and this strengthens our glutes and quads."

She points out that you can do bodyweight squats against the wall if you're not comfortable with air squats. Just be sure to keep your weight in your heels as you sit back and low.

**PLANK**

"Planks work the whole body if you do them right," Jones says. "They are great for developing core stability and strengthening your upper and lower body at the same time."

You can modify a plank by standing and placing your hands against a wall, bench or desk that won't move from under you, or you could take a kneeling plank as well.

**JUMPING JACKS**

"When it comes to cardio exercises, I love to go old-school," Jones says. "Think about the moves from P.E. class."

Jumping jacks are one of her favorite moves for getting your heart rate up quickly. You can also try jumping rope if you have the space.

**BURPEES**

Jones says burpees are a trainer favorite because they're a cardio and strength exercise in one, working the entire body. If you're not comfortable taking your burpees down to the floor, you can put your hands on a bench or table that won't move from under you. Just hop your legs back, open them to a jack, close and hop back in toward your hands.

**CORE AND MAT EXERCISES**

Jones says there are a million variations of crunches and sit-ups, which can easily and safely be done anywhere in the house. These exercises help strengthen your abdominals and back, which helps with everyday functionality.

**LUNGES**

Lunges target the lower body, but Jones says you can easily add a shoulder press or biceps curl to work the entire body if you're short on time.

She likes lunges

KEEP YOUR BODY IN A STRAIGHT LINE FROM YOUR HEAD TO YOUR HEELS WHILE PLANKING.

because you can take them forward, backward and to the side, all of which work your glutes and leg muscles differently.

**TURN THESE MOVES INTO A WORKOUT**

You can easily make these moves into a HIIT (high-intensity interval training) workout. Start timing 20 to 30 seconds per move—with a few seconds of rest in between—and see how you feel. (Pro tip: Download a free interval timer app on your phone to make things easy.) You can repeat the series once or multiple times for a serious total-body workout.

Tabata is another common format used for bodyweight workouts. This involves doing a move for 20 seconds, resting for 10 seconds and then repeating for eight rounds—about 4 minutes. You can repeat this process multiple times until you reach your time goal. This is Carrie Underwood's favorite way to work up a sweat when she's short on time. Check out Jones's IGTV account for workout inspiration.

Additionally, you'll want to make time to stretch regularly. Most of us don't have an ergonomic desk chair at home to help us maintain proper posture and are likely working from a couch or uncomfortable hard-backed chair instead. Stretching is a great way to de-stress, relieve shoulder or back pain and help your body feel its best.

Your home is a great option for workouts. You'll have more time to exercise than you do at the gym, and it's free! You can still take care of your body and build a regular workout routine that strengthens your muscles. Practicing mindfulness and movement through exercise is a great way to find balance and practice self-care—two things that can make you feel healthier and happier. ●

# Perfect Pairings

## Boost your fitness with workouts that complement each other.

**BY CINDY KUZMA**

Obsessed with cycling? Adore weight training? Congratulations on finding a workout you love! But if your routine is one-note, you're likely missing out on a whole symphony of benefits that other types of exercise offer. It can even be harmful. "Doing the same thing all the time can be hard on your body," says Chris Gagliardi, a personal trainer and a health coach certified by the American Council on Exercise.

Mixing it up with a different workout a few days a week creates a well-rounded program that works all your muscles, addresses imbalances and helps prevent injury. Here, three exercise pairings that go particularly well together.

### CYCLING + YOGA

Yoga works wonders for flexibility and strength, but it may not get your heart pumping hard enough, says Gagliardi. So pair your practice with pedaling, which will boost your heart rate and benefit your cardiovascular system. Cycling also works your hamstrings (which many yoga poses don't target) and gives your upper body and back (places all those Sun Salutations do tax) a break. Try a spin class, or hit the trail or road, where you'll reap the mood-boosting benefits of nature too.

Meanwhile, yoga poses strengthen the back, core and upper body—areas that cycling tends to neglect. What's more, the deep breaths and mind-body connection provide a good balance to the blaring tunes of a spin class, and can help you stay centered while navigating traffic on road rides.

### SWIMMING + PLYOMETRICS

Hitting the pool offers a total-body workout that boosts cardiovascular fitness and protects against chronic conditions like diabetes and heart disease. But there's one component it lacks: impact. Because of that, it doesn't help you maintain strong bones the way weight-bearing exercises like walking and running do.

The ideal solution? Balance swimming with explosive moves like box jumps, skips and bounds. These exercises can be intense, so start small and progress. For instance, practice side lunges for a while, then work your way up to side-to-side hops.

If weight-bearing plyo moves are already part of your regimen, make some of your leaps in the pool. The supportive nature of the water can give your joints a break. Plus, it'll help you hit your cardio targets.

### RUNNING + STRENGTH TRAINING

The constant pounding of shoes on pavement leaves runners at risk for overuse injuries like Achilles tendinitis and runner's knee. Doing leg and core exercises such as squats, lunges and crunches can reduce your risk of these ailments by making your muscles, joints and connective tissues stronger and more resilient. Add in moves to tone the upper-body muscles that running doesn't target, as well.

On the flip side, there's good reason for those who hang out near the weight rack to venture toward the treadmills, Gagliardi says. Resistance training typically doesn't get your heart rate up enough to count toward the recommended 150 weekly minutes of moderate-intensity cardio.

Because running is so vigorous, you can get by with just 75 weekly minutes of huffing and puffing.

# Here's One Way Women Are Stronger Than Men

See ya later, Chad! Women can exercise longer than men can before getting tired, research shows.

**BY AMANDA MACMILLAN**

Ladies, you now have some science-backed bragging rights: Women can exercise for longer than men before getting tired, according to a scientific review.

It's not because women are stronger; men are generally more powerful than comparably fit females. But here's the catch: Women's muscles tend to be more resistant to fatigue than men's, which means they can perform at the same relative intensity for a longer duration.

"I may not be able to bench-press the same amount of weight as a big muscle-bound guy, but if you ask us both to perform a contraction at 100 percent of our maximum strength and sustain it as long as we can, I should be able to outperform him," says study author Sandra Hunter, PhD, associate professor of exercise science at Marquette University.

The 2016 paper, published in the journal *Medicine & Science in Sports & Exercise,* highlights a big problem in the scientific community: Many studies—including research on physical activity and performance—are only done on men. But exercise routines designed for best results in men may not be as well suited for women, suggests the small number of studies that have involved both genders. Hunter reviewed these studies in her paper and encouraged scientists to add to them with their future work.

"The bottom line of training or rehab is that you have to fatigue a muscle in order to increase its strength," Hunter explains. "So if men and women fatigue differently, they should be treated differently." This is especially important during physical therapy after injuries, surgery or a diagnosis of osteoarthritis, she adds.

Research has shown, for example, that women retain more strength in their legs after running a marathon or cycling for a long period of time. In other tests, women have been able to hold isometric contractions (like making a fist or flexing a bicep) for longer durations than men when performed at the same percentage of their maximum strength.

These measures aren't just relevant in lab settings. "We perform these types of subtle, static contractions all day long," Hunter says. "They're important for holding us up while we're standing or sitting upright. And we know women can essentially do them for longer than men."

Gender advantages vary by activity, as well. Women burn more fat and fewer carbohydrates than men during sustained exercise, "which sets them up to perform, potentially, for longer periods of time if they're going at the same intensity as men," Hunter says. But women have smaller hearts, smaller muscles and more body fat than men, so it can be hard for them to keep up with men in a sport like running. In an activity like swimming, those differences matter less. "Look at Diana Nyad," Hunter says. "The first person to swim from Cuba to Florida [without a protective cage] was a woman."

So does that mean we can declare women the tougher sex? "It's very tempting to say that, isn't it?" Hunter says. But toughness can be

measured in a lot of different ways, she adds, and women certainly don't come out on top in all of them.

There's also plenty that science still doesn't know, which is one of the main points of Hunter's new research. Existing studies do show that women have the upper hand when it comes to fatigability. But they've only looked at very specific tasks or specific limbs, she says, and it's hard to take those findings and make broader assumptions.

The answer, says Hunter, is that more research is needed. Significant progress has been made in the last 20 years, and women are certainly better represented now than they used to be, both in scientific studies and in real-world athletic arenas. "To be clear, the best woman probably won't ever be able to outrun the best man, simply because of physiological differences," Hunter says. "But for many years those differences have been overestimated because we haven't had the best genetic pool of women competing against the best genetic pool of men."

Hunter is confident these performance gaps will continue to narrow as women's sports programs grow and improve. She also hopes her research encourages a future where each gender's strengths and weaknesses are taken into account by scientists, coaches and health professionals. "If we can give women care that's tailored to them," she says, "we can really help them reach their full potential." ●

WEIGHTS, DUMBBELLS AND RESISTANCE BANDS ARE GREAT FOR WORKING HAND MUSCLES.

# Get a Grip

## Who knew that better health was literally in your hands? Here's what to know—and how to boost your grip strength.

**BY K. ALEISHA FETTERS, CSCS**

Hand-grip strength is about more than opening pickle jars with ease. It's also about your longevity and quality of life. Research has linked low grip strength to an increased risk for cognitive impairment, fractures, falls, depression, sleep problems, type 2 diabetes and premature death.

One long-term study published in the *Lancet* even found grip strength to be a better predictor of the odds of dying from cardiovascular disease—or from any cause—than blood pressure. Why? Grip strength is a reliable marker of overall muscle mass, which is critical to the function of every system in your body, explains lead author Darryl P. Leong, MPH, PhD.

Muscle size and strength tend to decline as you age, starting as early as your 30s. But doing resistance exercises that work your body's major muscle groups can prevent or help reverse that loss. Plus, the more weight you're able to hold on to and lift, the more muscle mass you'll be able to build, says Michele Olson, PhD, senior clinical professor of sport science and physical education at Huntingdon College in Montgomery, Alabama. Here are three exercises that Olson recommends:

**FARMER'S CARRY**
Stand with your feet about hip-width apart with a pair of dumbbells on the floor by the outsides of your feet. Squat down, and, keeping your back flat and abs pulled in tight, grab a weight in each hand and stand up, arms by your sides, palms facing your thighs. From here, walk forward until your hands feel like they're about to give out, then lower the weights to the floor. Work up to three reps.

**DEAD LIFT**
Stand with your feet about hip-width apart and a pair of dumbbells by your toes, placed perpendicular to your body. Push your butt and hips back and bend forward at the waist, keeping your back flat and abs pulled in tight, with your knees just slightly bent. Pick up the weights, palms facing the front of your thighs, arms straight, and push through your heels to stand back up (keep your arms long and close to the front of your thighs). Slowly reverse the motion and lower the weights to the floor. Work up to three sets of 8 to 12 reps.

**HOLLOW-BODY HANG**
Grab a sturdy overhead bar with an overhand grip, thumbs wrapped under the bar, hands slightly wider than shoulder-width apart. Pull your shoulder blades down and back and raise your feet off the floor so your body forms an elongated C shape. Hold it for as long as possible, keeping your arms and core engaged. Work up to doing four 30-second holds.

**WHAT ABOUT HAND-GRIP TOOLS?**
Isolating your hand grip with squeeze balls and other trainers won't directly protect you from chronic disease, says Olson. But focusing in on grip with a special tool can get you more results from moves like carries, dead lifts, and hangs that will help improve your overall muscle mass and health. Try doing three sets of 10 reps with a hand-grip trainer at the beginning of every workout. ●

# Power Center

Your core is so much more than meets the mirror, in ways that go beyond muscle deep. Here's how to make yours its healthiest yet, outside and in.

**BY TULA KARRAS**

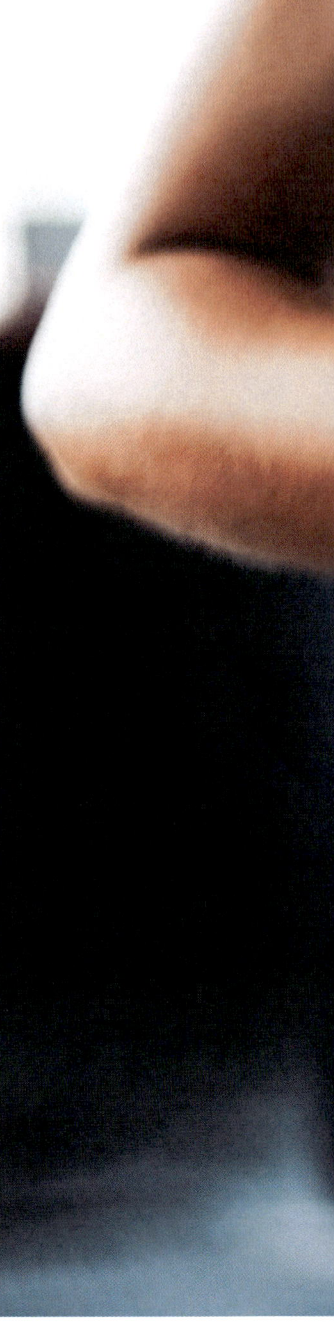

**OPTIMIZE YOUR ENERGY FLOW**
"Your core is the foundation for everything when it comes to movement," says Peter Ronai, a clinical professor of exercise science at Sacred Heart University in Connecticut. "Any activity that involves the arms or lower body uses the core as an axis." Your core encompasses not just the abdominals—the internal and external obliques along your sides, the rectus abdominis down the center, and the deeper transverse abdominis that wraps the waist—but all the muscles front and back, from the shoulder girdle to the pelvis and even the upper third of the thigh (yes, all that!). "The stronger and more stabilized your core, the more forceful any movement can be because you aren't leaking energy through the body's kinetic chain, its system of movement," Ronai says. His three-move series works your core as one dynamic unit. Do as many reps as you can with good form of curl-ups (cross arms over chest) and bird dogs (on all fours, alternate lifting opposite arm and leg), then five to ten 10-second side planks (on right, then left).

**KNOW YOUR GOAL STANDARDS**
How fit is your core? If you can do 30 to 36 curl-ups (bringing only shoulder blades off the mat) before stopping, it's in pretty good shape, according to the American Council on Exercise. Do more and you're above average. As for waist size, the latest from the American Heart Association suggests 35 inches or less for women is best for cutting your health risks, although researchers noted that more study is needed to understand how waist circumference affects stroke risk and how it impacts various racial and ethnic groups. Along with a healthy diet, high intensity interval training can help because it burns calories faster than other forms of exercise, says Ron Snarr, PhD, a kinesiologist at Georgia Southern University.

**MIND YOUR BACK**
The six and a half hours a day adults sit, on average, can sap core muscles, especially if you hunch. The slump can cause frontal core muscles to shorten and tighten, while back core muscles are elongating and not firing enough. "When we stay in misalignment for hours, we hardwire imbalances into the muscles and joints and compromise strength and function," Ronai says. Realign by lifting the top of your sternum up and bringing your shoulder blades down your rib cage. You also want to activate the thoracic (upper) spine and scapula muscles regularly, Ronai says: Squeeze your shoulder blades together while sitting, do seated rows (with or without weights), and draw back your chin (if it juts) throughout the day.

**HIGH-TECH OPTIONS**
While these options are not for everyone, some cutting-edge in-office treatments offer alternative ways to tone and trim. "If you're treating the abs, a 30-minute Emsculpt session is the equivalent of 20,000 contractions," says dermatologist Jared Jagdeo, MD, chief medical officer of Ever/Body in New York City, of the muscle-building device that uses electromagnetic energy to elicit those reps. A variation known as Emsculpt Neo adds a bit of fat reduction as well, also using radio frequency energy to destroy fat cells. Other devices, such as CoolSculpting Elite, eliminate those fat cells by freezing them. To smooth the skin, Melissa Doft, MD, a New York plastic surgeon, is a fan of the combination of

microneedling (tiny needle pricks to stimulate collagen and elastin) and Radiesse, a hyaluronic filler. "The pairing can reduce the appearance of cellulite and tighten loose skin," she says.

**FREE YOUR MIND**
Doing a regular de-stress is as potent a part of your game plan as planks. "High levels of steady stress produce a sustained stream of the hormone cortisol, which reduces AMPK, an enzyme that regulates our fat and carbohydrate metabolism," says Deena Adimoolam, MD, an endocrinologist in New York. "When AMPK drops, so does fat metabolism, which over time leads to an increase in visceral fat." That visceral fat within your middle is the deep-down kind that surrounds the organs and messes with your health. "Abdominal fat secretes inflammatory biomarkers that can eventually lead to heart disease, as well as increased risk of diabetes," says Tiffany Powell-Wiley, MD, who cowrote the American Heart Association's recent recommendation for waist measurement to be part of annual check-ups. Besides meditation, try to work in a 20-minute dose of nature: Researchers from the University of Michigan found that people who spend 20 to 30 minutes sitting or walking in greenery a few times a week significantly reduce their cortisol levels. ●

BANDS CAN CREATE ADDITIONAL TENSION DURING WARM-UP EXERCISES, ACTIVATING MUSCLES FOR A MORE STRENUOUS WORKOUT.

# MINI-BAND MAGIC

Use this routine to ramp up your total-body strength—in just 15 minutes!

**BY ROZALYNN S. FRAZIER**

The mini resistance band doesn't get nearly enough credit. But this small, portable piece of elastic is mightier than you think, providing external tension on your muscles to make them (and you!) work harder. And according to Le Sweat founder Charlee Atkins (pictured), who designed this six-move circuit, it's not only great for total-body toning—it "also adds more variety to workouts than traditional bodyweight exercises provide." Bonus: It's beginner-friendly, too!

**DO EACH EXERCISE FOR 40 SECONDS** back-to-back without rest.

**COMPLETE 3 TOTAL SETS,** resting for 60 seconds between each.

**AIM TO DO THE CIRCUIT 3 TO 5 TIMES** a week.

## Supine Extension

**(A)** Lie face-up with a mini resistance band around your arches, knees bent at 90 degrees. Lift head and shoulders, and place hands lightly on the back of your head. **(B)** Extend left leg straight out; left heel should be about one inch above the ground. Hold for one breath. Bring left leg back in and then extend right leg straight out; continue alternating.

## Band Dead Lift

**(A)** Place a mini resistance band under the ball of right foot, holding the opposite end in both hands. With a slight bend in knees, hinge at hips, lowering torso until hands are at or below knees. **(B)** With control, rise to standing. Lower back to A and repeat.

## Half-Kneeling Pulldown

**(A)** Place a mini resistance band around wrists. Kneel on right knee with left knee up and left foot planted. Keep abs tight. Extend arms straight up, palms facing forward. **(B)** Keeping elbows close to body, pull arms straight down to the base of the ribs while pulling the band apart. Return to A and repeat.

## Push-up + Superwoman

**(A)** With a mini resistance band around ankles, get into a high plank with feet hip-width apart and hands directly underneath shoulders. **(B)** Keeping elbows in, lower to ground. **(C)** Extend arms straight out; then squeeze glutes to lift chest and thighs. Lower back to ground, then push back up to A. Repeat sequence.

## Squat-Pulse Combo

**(A)** Place a mini resistance band just below knees and stand tall, feet shoulder-width apart. Push hips back, bend knees and lower into a squat with hands clasped and extended in front of your chest. **(B)** Step right foot out to the right side and then back in to A. **(C)** Maintaining position, repeat movement with left foot. Rise back to standing; repeat sequence.

**WORK UP TO MORE RESISTANCE**

Buy a band set with multiple resistances so you can keep challenging yourself as you get stronger.

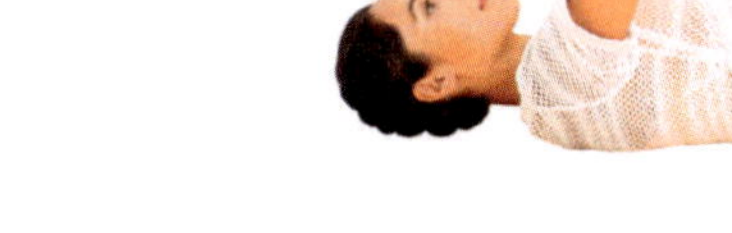

A

## Sit-up + Row

**(A)** Lie face-up with knees bent, feet flat on ground, and arms extended straight up, with a mini resistance band around thumbs. **(B)** Keeping arms extended, raise torso to move into a V shape. **(C)** Pull right elbow down and back until wrist is at your ribs. Return right arm to full extension; repeat on left side. Lower back to A and repeat.

# ARMED WITH STRENGTH

Work your upper body with these creative, challenging exercises—no weights required.

BY MALLORY CREVELING

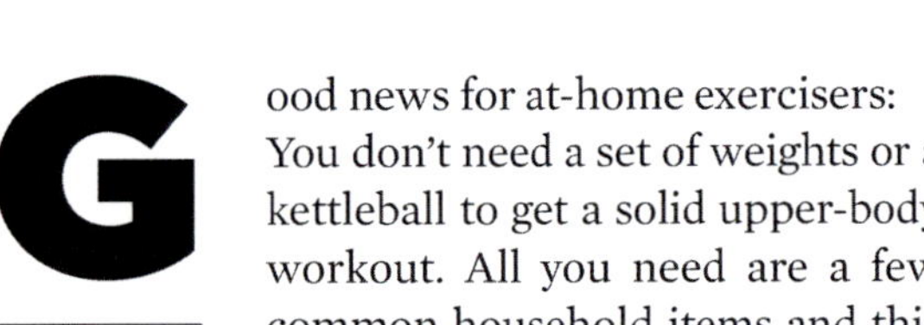

Good news for at-home exercisers: You don't need a set of weights or a kettleball to get a solid upper-body workout. All you need are a few common household items and this workout from NASM-certified trainer Jennifer Romanelli (shown), co-owner of Trooper Fitness in New York City.

Bodyweight exercises not only build muscle but can also power you through your days. "Tweak your training to what you want to do in your life—make it work for you," Romanelli says. (For her, that means carrying a toddler in one arm and a stroller in the other while walking up five flights!)

Your sense of accomplishment will grow every time you do a few more push-ups or hold your plank a little longer, and that progress will motivate you to work through the challenges, Romanelli says.

## Shoots

**(A)** Place hands on two chairs and walk feet back to a plank position, shoulders over wrists. Bend elbows 45 degrees and lower chest toward chairs to perform a push-up. Press back up to plank. Drive hands into chairs; lift hips and feet off the ground and sweep them underneath you, landing in a reverse plank with legs straight out in front, heels on the ground and arms straight.
**(B)** Bend elbows 45 degrees and lower butt toward floor to perform a triceps dip. Press back up, driving hands into the chairs and lifting hips and feet off floor to sweep them underneath you and back to a plank position for the push-up. Continue alternating between push-up and dip.

+

RESIST SHRUGGING YOUR SHOULDERS—KEEP THEM NEUTRAL, WITH YOUR NECK RELAXED.

A

B

## Modified Handstand Push-up

**(A)** Place hands on floor and feet on a chair behind you, so body forms an L shape. **(B)** Bend elbows and lower head toward floor, between hands. Press back up and repeat.

A

Keep your legs straight.

B

## Bat Wing

**(A)** Start seated, knees straight and heels planted, leaning slightly backward, with elbows bent and placed on towels slightly behind you. **(B)** Drive elbows outward, lowering back toward floor. Then, squeezing shoulder blades together, pull elbows back toward center as you sit up taller. Repeat.

A

B

## Towel Chest Fly

**(A)** Start in a modified plank position (on knees), each hand on a towel or glider in front of you. **(B)** Maintaining a modified plank, with pelvis tucked slightly forward, glutes and abs engaged, drive towels straight out to the sides, keeping a slight bend in the elbows. Press up as you slide the towels back under your shoulders. Repeat.

Keep your back straight.

A

B

## Triceps Extension

**(A)** Place hands on a chair and walk feet back to a plank position. (Keep feet wide to make it easier, closer together to increase the challenge.) **(B)** Squeezing elbows toward each other, bend them straight back, lowering upper body toward floor.

## The Drill

**CIRCUIT 1: PYRAMID**
Perform **Modified Handstand Push-ups** and **Shoots** "pyramid" style, starting at 2 reps each and building to 4, 6, 8 and 10, then back down: 2 **Handstand Push-ups**, 2 **Shoots**, 4 **Handstand Push-ups**, 4 **Shoots**, etc.

**CIRCUIT 2: TRI SET**
Do 3 sets
**Towel Chest Fly**
12 reps
**Triceps Extension**
10 reps
**Bat Wing**
15 to 20 reps

**CIRCUIT 3: AB FINISHER**
Do 3 sets
**Towel Ab Rollout**
15 reps
**Adductor Plank**
30 seconds each side

## Towel Ab Rollout

**(A)** Start in a forearm plank position, shoulders right over elbows and both feet on towels. **(B)** Maintaining a strong plank, glide feet back so shoulders come behind elbows. Then pull forward, shoulders returning back over elbows. Continue moving back and forth.

## Adductor Plank

Start with your right elbow on the floor, and then place left foot on top of chair and right foot under the seat, getting into a side plank position, hips stacked and right shoulder directly over right elbow. Keeping body in a straight line from shoulder to feet, hold for 30 seconds. Switch sides.

CHAPTER 3

# REST AND RECHARGE

From taming post-workout inflammation to ensuring a restful night's sleep, what comes after exercise is just as important.

# STRENGTH THROUGH SLEEP

Research has shown that regular strength training and deep slumber are perfect bedfellows.

**BY EMILY JOSHU**

A good night's sleep is one of the most elusive aspects of full-body wellness. Sleep deprivation leads many of us to struggle to feel rested and attentive throughout the day, and the body needs sleep to restore itself and protect against illnesses, as well as ensure muscle health. Science suggests that picking up some light dumbbells or going for a run could be key to a restful night of sleep and waking in the morning without slamming the snooze button.

Research has shown that engaging in several types of exercise can increase levels of testosterone in both men and women, which is directly linked to nighttime sleep quality. Healthy levels of testosterone build more muscle than low levels, which can also be achieved with strength training. Some of the earliest research, a 1983 study in the

+ RESEARCHERS FOUND THAT LIFTING WEIGHTS IN THE MORNING HELPED SUBJECTS FALL ASLEEP FASTER AND SLEEP MORE SOUNDLY THAT NIGHT.

*European Journal of Applied Physiology and Occupational Physiology,* found that testosterone levels in men increased significantly after weight lifting. Additionally, a 2012 comparative study in the *European Journal of Applied Physiology* discovered a link between higher testosterone levels and men who exercised regularly compared with men who were sedentary. And a 2016 study of obese men, published in the *Journal of Clinical Biochemistry and Nutrition*, found that regular exercise did more to increase testosterone levels than simply losing weight. While men generally produce more testosterone than women do, women also produce it.

The relationship between testosterone and nighttime sleep quality hinges on slow wave sleep, also known as deep sleep. It occurs during phase 3 of sleep, which is the deepest phase of non-rapid eye movement (NREM) sleep. During this phase, the sleeper stays relatively still but can be susceptible to dreaming and sleepwalking. "It's a very aggressive form of sleep, so even if you only sleep a few hours, it forces its way into the night," says Matthew Ebben, PhD, associate professor in the department of sleep medicine at Weill Cornell Medical College. This kind of sleep can be difficult to wake up from. Additionally, slow wave sleep has a rebound effect to help the body catch up if it has missed out on this crucial sleep stage—for example, if you stay up too late one night but then fall back into regular sleep habits the next day. During periods of deep sleep, a growth hormone crucial for building muscle is secreted. Sleep also allows the muscles to relax, which can reduce tension and pain; that's why you may wake up sore and tense after a sleepless night. Long-term lack of sleep has also been linked to the development of chronic pain.

Certain conditions, such as obstructive sleep apnea, can result in difficulty getting to slow wave sleep, since individuals experience fragmented sleep patterns where they frequently stop breathing. So while simply not getting enough sleep can leave you drained and unwilling to exercise, the behind-the-scenes process of slow wave sleep has a greater influence on how you feel the next day.

Slow wave sleep, however, gradually declines with age. People generally experience the highest levels of slow wave sleep during childhood, and the levels decrease as we get older. By age 60, men have likely lost all slow wave sleep. However, Ebben says, this type of sleep declines faster for men, who have significantly more testosterone than women. A 1997 comparative study in the *Journal of Sleep Research,* for example, found that significant reductions in slow wave sleep occurred in men in their 30s, while it did not diminish for women. This suggests that the gender difference in slow wave sleep may emerge between age 30 and 40 in young adults. Additional research published in the *Journal of Clinical Endocrinology & Metabolism* found that by age 45, testosterone starts falling by 1 percent a year. Other research suggests that could start even earlier. In men, low testosterone has been linked not only to sleep disturbances but also to low

energy, depressed mood, and loss of muscle and bone strength. "This isn't something that you can really do that much about," Ebben says. "Particularly men, as they get older, they lose the ability to generate this type of sleep, and they also have a reduction in the prodution of that human growth hormone. It appears that there's a relationship between these things."

**A CHALLENGING WORKOUT CAN IMPACT HOW** much time you spend actually sleeping while in bed rather than just being awake. "All different forms of exercise improve what we call sleep efficiency," Ebben says. "The ability to maintain sleep during the night, sleep efficiency, is represented in terms of the proportion of time spent in bed over sleep time. For example, somebody with 95 percent sleep efficiency is sleeping 95 percent of the time that they're in bed." A sleep efficiency score of 85 percent or greater—the equivalent of just under seven hours of total sleep with eight hours of time trying to fall asleep—is considered a good score, though some people are naturally able to fall asleep faster and sleep more soundly than others. Stress, pain and illness; noises such as a partner's snoring; and diet can have a negative impact on overall sleep efficiency. A 2010 study in the journal *Psychosomatic Medicine* suggests that a couple's personal interactions throughout the day could affect sleep efficiency. For example, fewer negative interactions throughout the day suggested a higher likelihood of optimal sleep efficiency.

One of the most effective exercises to boost testosterone and sleep quality is resistance training, which involves strengthening the muscles with free weights, medicine balls, weight machines, resistance bands, or suspension equipment. Starting a strength-training routine, research suggests, could improve a person's sleep quality. A 2005 pilot study in the *Journal of Sports Science & Medicine* found that "resistance training led to improvements in sleep as measured by a self-report sleep questionnaire," the authors wrote. Participants completed a one-circuit resistance-training routine comprised of bench presses, leg presses, leg extensions, rowing, shoulder presses, and arm curls for 10 to 12 reps each. A 2020 study in the journal *Scientific Reports* found that resistance training improved total sleep time and sleep efficiency in patients undergoing hemodialysis, a treatment for kidney failure.

**Sleep allows the muscles to relax, which can reduce tension and pain; that's why you may wake up sore and tense after a sleepless night.**

If you're new to strength training, consider light, adjustable dumbbells, or use a water jug in place of a medicine ball. Even just your body weight can be an effective strength-training tool, with moves that target your core and lower-body muscles. Limit strength workouts to 45 minutes, and make sure to rest for at least 60 seconds between sets. This helps reduce the risk of fatigue and injury in beginners.

You don't have to exclusively hit the weights or the resistance band to get a better night's rest, though. "All kinds of exercise have been shown to improve nighttime sleep quality in general," Ebben says. In a recent study of 23,600 German adults published in *Preventive Medicine Reports,* researchers found that any muscle-strengthening exercise is associated with a reduced prevalence of "poor" or "very poor" sleep. Additionally, a 2018 review in the *Journal of Science and Medicine in Sport* suggests that sleep deprivation can impair overall muscle strength. A study of more than 75,000 postmenopausal women conducted by the Sleep Research Society found that the more physical activity the women got in during the day, the better they slept at night. The researchers found that women who were getting 7.5 to 17.5 hours of activity per week were more likely to sleep more than six hours, and those who were getting more than 7.5 hours a week of activity were 7 to 15 percent less likely to have restless sleep.

High-intensity interval training (HIIT) has also been shown to increase testosterone levels, which can lead to better sleep. One 2012 comparative study in the *Journal of Endocrinological Investigation* found that men who completed interval training with 90 seconds of interspersed treadmill running boosted their testosterone levels significantly more than those who ran for 45 minutes straight. Another study, from 2013, published in the *European Journal of Applied Physiology,* found that taking DHEA supplements along with five sessions of two-minute cycling exercises increased testosterone levels in both younger and older men. For a low-intensity alternative, preliminary research also points to yoga to get a better night's sleep and reduce stress, especially for certain populations who typically experience sleep disruptions, such as women, the elderly, people with type 2 diabetes, and children with autism spectrum disorder. A 2015 report from the Centers for Disease Control and Prevention showed that 55 percent of yoga practitioners reported improved sleep, and more than 85 percent reported overall reduced stress. A 2020 clinical trial published in *Psychiatria Danubina* found that yoga lessened symptoms of depression and anxiety while improving sleep quality among menopausal women. Additionally, a 2013 study in the *Indian Journal of Psychiatry* found that when elderly populations practiced yoga, it improved both their sleep quality and quality of life.

**WHILE EXERCISE AND STRENGTH WORKOUTS HAVE** been proven to foster better, more restful sleep, other lifestyle influences can also help you get a better night's rest, including sleep hygiene. The term refers to the environment in which a person is sleeping, as well as their daily routines. For example, someone with strong sleep hygiene might have a fixed bedtime and waking time and a comfortable, dark bedroom, and might exercise around the same

THE L-THEANINE IN MATCHA TEA HELPS CALM YOUR SENSES, SOOTHE YOUR NERVES, AND RELAX YOU BEFORE BED.

time every day. Reserving the last 30 minutes of the day for winding down and avoiding electronics can also cultivate strong sleep hygiene by putting the body in a relaxed mood. Additionally, doing anything before bed that increases body temperature has been shown to help with sleep quality. While this includes exercising just before bedtime, taking a hot shower or drinking a steaming cup of tea can also increase slow wave sleep.

CBD products and melatonin supplements have become popular interventions for some who want to alleviate anxiety around bedtime and fall asleep faster, though Ebben cautions against using them as primary treatments. "I don't think CBD needs to be part of the discussion of good quality sleep. I think there are other things that people should do that are much more important than worrying about CBD or melatonin," he says. "You can help yourself much more by exercising and working on your schedule than you can by taking something out of a vape or bottle. If you can reduce your anxiety through exercise, that's going to help your nighttime sleep quality."

When cultivating a better night's sleep, forming a routine is a crucial first step. "Consistency is king when it comes to sleep," Ebben says. "You generally want to go to sleep and wake up around the same time every day, because we have what are called circadian rhythms, which are body rhythms that predict when you're going to sleep and when you're waking up. If you're moving around your awake time and your sleep time, it affects those circadian rhythms—they don't know when to prepare your body for sleep and when to prepare your body for wakefulness." He also recommends limiting the amount of non-sleep time you spend in bed. If you're having trouble falling asleep, consider getting up and walking around, and try to limit your Netflix-in-bed time.

If you're just getting started lifting weights, trying yoga, or sweating it out with HIIT, Ebben recommends going slow at first and consulting with a healthcare provider to assess your skill level and set a starting point. Then, with that in mind, practice consistency with your workouts and bedtime routines. ●

# 4 Ways to Help Your Body Recover Between Workouts—and 1 Thing to Avoid

Try recovery sessions between workouts to feel better and fast-track your fitness goals.

**BY DANIELLE KOSECKI**

High-intensity interval training still ranks as the "it" workout, according to the American College of Sports Medicine. If reading this makes your quads quake, take heart. Recovery studios are catching on, with CrossFitters and spinners as well as elliptical lovers and barre enthusiasts getting on board. "People assumed that it was the workout that yielded the benefit, but it's really how well you recuperate between sessions that gets results," says Aaron Drogoszewski, CPT, the cofounder of Recover, a New York City–based recovery studio.

Any exercise that challenges you generates microtears in your muscle fibers—and when they repair themselves, you get stronger. Recovery techniques are intended to help speed you through this process. Check out these four to try—and one to skip.

**TECHNIQUES TO TRY**

**Sauna**

Traditional saunas use high heat (around 185°F) to help increase circulation in your body, expediting the delivery of oxygen- and nutrient-rich blood to muscles. Infrared saunas emit light that can get deeper into your body than warmed air can, producing the same effects at a slightly more comfortable 140°. And some promising, though preliminary, research suggests that either may have benefits for decreasing post-workout pain or boosting performance during your next workout. Just remember your water bottle—dehydration can make soreness worse.

**Massage**

French researchers analyzed 99 studies comparing recovery strategies and found that massage reduced muscle soreness and fatigue better than other techniques. How does it work? One possibility: "Direct pressure activates pain receptors in muscles that send pain signals to the brain, which then sends down morphine-like compounds that decrease that pain," says exercise physiologist David Behm, PhD. Massage may also improve range of motion, reduce tightness and promote blood flow to muscles to speed recovery. You can DIY with a foam roller or percussive massager, like the Theragun.

**Active Recovery**

Watch the Tour de France and you'll notice that riders will finish a leg of the race and immediately get on a stationary bike for a light spin. That's active recovery. Cooling down with light exercise can help you feel more rested and less sore for your next sweat session, according to a study in the *Journal of Strength and Conditioning Research.* Active recovery keeps circulation elevated, which speeds up the removal of lactate, a by-product of exercise that can interfere with muscle repair processes, says Behm. Doing 6 to 10 minutes of low-intensity cycling, rowing or jogging at the tail end of your workout is ideal.

**Stretching**

Important for fitness? Yes. For recovery? Less so. In a Cochrane review, post-exercise stretching alleviated soreness by only 1 to 4 percent. (And a pre-workout stretch impacts how you'll feel during your workout, not after.) But don't scrap the practice. It may help you feel less tight. "Stretching is important for your functional range of motion," says Malachy McHugh, PhD, director of research at the Nicholas Institute of Sports Medicine and Athletic Trauma in New York City. "It makes the muscle more compliant and stronger in a stretched position"—all important factors for your workout.

**TECHNIQUE TO SKIP**

**Ice Bath**

Athletes have long been plunging their legs into ice water as a way to slow down the immune system's inflammatory response to exercise. Research does support that it can reduce how sore and tired your muscles feel, but it's possible the tried-and-true technique works too well. Studies show that muscles can't repair without some inflammation; it kick-starts the healing process. So when you cut it short, you may be delaying the recovery process and stunting strength gains. ●

+
A 2021 ANIMAL STUDY FOUND THAT MASSAGE THERAPY DOUBLED THE RATE OF MUSCLE RECOVERY.

# SWEET TREATS FOR SLUMBER

Wind down at night with these delicious desserts that are packed with sleep-friendly ingredients.

## Strawberries & Cream Pops

**ACTIVE**: 30 minutes
**TOTAL**: 6¾ hours
**TO MAKE AHEAD**: Freeze for up to 1 week.
**EQUIPMENT**: Six 3-ounce freezer-pop molds

*A glossy compote swirled with softened frozen yogurt gives these pops Creamsicle vibes. Strawberries are a natural source of melatonin.*

**1 pound strawberries, hulled and quartered**
**2 teaspoons lemon juice**
**2 teaspoons granulated sugar**
**1¼ cups vanilla frozen yogurt**

**1.** Combine strawberries, lemon juice and sugar in a medium saucepan. Cook over medium heat, stirring, until the sugar is dissolved and the fruit has broken down, 8 to 10 minutes. Transfer the mixture to a bowl and refrigerate, uncovered, until completely cooled, about 30 minutes.
**2.** Let frozen yogurt soften for a few minutes at room temperature. Stir with a sturdy flexible spatula until pliable. (If it gets too soft, return to the freezer for a few minutes to firm up slightly.)
**3.** Alternate layers of 1 tablespoon each of the frozen yogurt and compote into each of six 3-ounce freezer-pop molds until they're almost full. Using a skewer or chopstick, gently stir to create a swirled pattern. Insert sticks. Freeze until solid, at least 6 hours or up to 1 week.

**SERVES 6:** 1 POP EACH
**CAL** 75, **FAT** 2G (SAT 1G), **CHOL** 5MG, **CARBS** 14G, **TOTAL SUGARS** 10G (ADDED 7G), **PROTEIN** 1G, **FIBER** 1G, **SODIUM** 16MG, **POTASSIUM** 111MG.

## "Chocomole" Pudding

**ACTIVE**: 15 minutes
**TOTAL**: 3¼ hours
**TO MAKE AHEAD**: Cover and refrigerate for up to 2 days. Stir before serving.

*Creamy avocados make this dairy-free and vegan dessert super rich. The omega-3 fatty acids in avocado can help improve your sleep quality.*

- **16 Medjool dates, pitted and coarsely chopped**
- **3 ripe avocados**
- **1 cup unsweetened almond milk or coconut milk beverage**
- **1 cup unsweetened cocoa powder**
- **¼ cup pure maple syrup or agave nectar**
- **1 tablespoon coconut oil**
- **1 teaspoon vanilla extract**
- **Pinch of sea salt, plus more for garnish**

**1.** Soak dates in 1 cup hot water until soft, 5 to 10 minutes. Drain.
**2.** Process the dates, avocados, milk beverage, cocoa, maple syrup (or agave), oil, vanilla and a pinch of salt in a food processor until very smooth and creamy.
**3.** Refrigerate until cold, about 3 hours. Serve garnished with a little extra sea salt, if desired.

**SERVES 6:** ½ CUP EACH
**CAL** 434, **FAT** 20G (SAT 5G), **CHOL** 0MG, **CARBS** 74G, **TOTAL SUGARS** 52G (ADDED 9G), **PROTEIN** 6G, **FIBER** 16G, **SODIUM** 54MG, **POTASSIUM** 1,212MG.

## Tart Cherry Nice Cream

**ACTIVE**: 10 min

**TOTAL**: 10 min

**TO MAKE AHEAD**: While the nice cream will have the best texture if served immediately, it can be stored in the freezer for up to 3 months. Let soften at room temperature for about an hour before serving.

*This easy vegan "nice cream"—made from only a few simple ingredients—is guaranteed to satisfy your sweet tooth and also deliver a boost of melatonin that may help you get a more restful night's sleep.*

- **3 ripe bananas, peeled, sliced and frozen**
- **2 cups frozen pitted sweet cherries**
- **1 cup frozen pitted tart cherries**
- **¼ cup unsweetened almond milk**

Combine bananas, sweet cherries, tart cherries and almond milk in a blender or food processor. Process until smooth, scraping down the sides as needed.

**SERVES 4:** 1 CUP EACH

**CAL** 145, **FAT** 1G (SAT 0G), **CHOL** 0MG, **CARBS** 36G, **TOTAL SUGARS** 23G (ADDED 0G), **PROTEIN** 2G, **FIBER** 4G, **SODIUM** 13MG, **POTASSIUM** 526MG.

## Banana Cream Pudding Parfait

**ACTIVE**: 40 minutes
**TOTAL**: 4 hours 40 minutes (including 3 hours chilling time)
**TO MAKE AHEAD**: Prepare through Step 5 up to 5 days ahead. Finish Step 6 and refrigerate the parfaits for up to 4 hours.

*Banana-infused milk is the base of this intensely flavored pudding. Folding it with whipped yogurt gives it a mousse-like texture. Layers of toasted hazelnuts add crunch. Bananas are chock full of magnesium, which helps the mind and body relax before bed.*

### Banana Pudding

- **1½ cups reduced-fat milk plus 2 tablespoons, divided**
- **2 large or 3 small very ripe bananas, sliced**
- **1 envelope unflavored gelatin (2¼ teaspoons)**
- **½ cup sugar**
- **½ cup nonfat dry milk**
- **⅛ teaspoon kosher salt**
- **½ cup heavy cream**
- **½ cup reduced-fat plain Greek yogurt**
- **1½ teaspoons vanilla extract**

### Layers and Topping

- **3 medium firm ripe bananas, sliced**
- **¾ cup coarsely chopped toasted hazelnuts**

**1. To prepare pudding:** Bring 1½ cups milk and banana slices to a simmer in a small nonreactive saucepan (see Tips), then remove from heat. Cover and let stand for 1 hour. Or cool to room temperature, cover and refrigerate for up to 1 day.

**2.** Mix gelatin with the remaining 2 tablespoons milk in a medium bowl, stirring to break up any lumps. Set a fine-mesh sieve over the bowl.

**3.** Add sugar, dry milk and salt to the banana-milk mixture; cook, stirring, until the dry ingredients have dissolved and the milk is steaming hot (do not let it boil), about 5 minutes.

**4.** Pour the milk mixture through the sieve into the gelatin, pressing on the bananas to extract as much milk as possible without actually mashing the pulp through the sieve. (Use the leftover pulp in a smoothie or muffin batter, or discard.) Whisk until the gelatin is dissolved. Cover and refrigerate until firm and cold, at least three hours and up to five days.

**5.** Scrape the chilled pudding into the bowl of a stand mixer fitted with a whisk attachment and whip on medium-high. At first it will look something like cottage cheese, but continue beating until smooth, about 1 minute. Return the pudding to its original container. Combine cream, yogurt and vanilla in the bowl and beat on medium-high for 5 full minutes. Fold into the pudding.

**6. To assemble parfaits:** Spoon ¼ cup pudding into each of 6 parfait glasses. Top with 3 or 4 banana slices and 1½ tablespoons hazelnuts, then another layer of banana slices. Spoon on another ¼ cup pudding and top with the remaining banana slices and hazelnuts. (To learn how to brûlée the banana slices for the topping, see Tips.)

**SERVES 6:** ABOUT ½ CUP PUDDING & 2 TBSP. NUTS EACH

**CAL** 348, **FAT** 18G (SAT 6G), **CHOL** 35MG, **CARBS** 41G, **TOTAL SUGARS** 32G (ADDED 17G), **PROTEIN** 10G, **FIBER** 3G, **SODIUM** 100MG, **POTASSIUM** 517MG.

### TIPS

**Use nonreactive bowls or pans**—stainless-steel, enamel-coated, nonstick or glass—when cooking with acidic foods (citrus, berries, tomatoes) to prevent the food from reacting with the dish. Reactive cookware (aluminum and cast-iron) can impart off colors and/or flavors.

**Brûléed banana slices**—sliced banana with a layer of caramelized sugar—make our banana pudding parfaits extra special for barely any extra calories. To make them, you'll need a small kitchen torch. Sprinkle a slice of banana with ½ teaspoon granulated sugar. Holding the flame 1 to 2 inches away, heat the sugar until it melts and browns. Let stand until crisp and cool.

# THE TRUTH ABOUT INFLAMMATION

Exercise-induced inflammation can be key for building muscle, but only in the right amounts. Here's how to hit the sweet spot.

**BY DEANNA PAI**

Inflammation is a buzzy topic these days. At high enough levels, it's considered a factor for everything from heart disease to acne, which is why it now has a bad reputation of sorts—hence the flood of all things anti-inflammatory. But inflammation serves an essential function in the body, not just as a collaborator with your immune response (its primary purpose) but also to help build muscle after a tough workout.

First off, what exactly is inflammation? At its most basic, "inflammation is the body's normal response to an infection or injury," says Beth Taylor, PhD, an associate professor of kinesiology at the University of Connecticut. "It's triggered by the immune system once the cells detect infection or injury." When your immune system is activated, it calls in a variety of immune cells to release hormones, increase blood flow and spur mucous membranes to release more fluid. That response leads to the classic signs of inflammation—think swelling, redness and tenderness. And that's a good thing. "All of these inflammatory responses serve the purpose of helping the body fight the foreign pathogen and repair tissue," Taylor says. Once the injury is resolved, the inflammation calls it quits.

Exercise can trigger the inflammatory response. "It's a stressor on the body. It stresses the muscles. It stresses the heart. So you have kind of a natural immune system response to it," Taylor explains. "We used to think it was just muscle damage that was the stress, but now what we realize is that it's really muscle contraction—just basic muscle contraction stimulates the immune system."

In the context of a workout, inflammation's goal is to help your body adapt to the exercise in a positive way by triggering the injury-

A LOW-IMPACT MEDICINE BALL ROUTINE CAN WORK YOUR ENTIRE BODY WITHOUT POUNDING ON YOUR JOINTS.

and-repair process. "That is, once the inflammation has resolved the damage done to skeletal muscle, the tissue will be repaired and likely the muscle will have improved function," says Stephen Cornish, PhD, a professor at the University of Manitoba who studies exercise and nutritional immunology. "This is the basis of why athletes train so rigorously to produce adaptations that will be beneficial for their performance," he adds.

The inflammation that happens after a workout is your body's normal response to the muscle contraction. On a cellular level, "the body releases factors such as cytokines, which trigger the release of immune cells—neutrophils and macrophages—to infiltrate muscle and repair injury," says Taylor. "In turn, this cycle of stress and repair induces increases in muscle mass, strength and function, which is what leads to health and performance gains following exercise."

This process can also suppress some inflammatory cytokines in a way that can reduce inflammation over time through a number of different pathways. It's more common when you're working with mild to moderate inflammation—soreness that subsides within a day or two. "Although soreness isn't always an indicator of whether a workout was 'good' or not, it is an indicator that you've introduced a new stimulus and your body is trying to repair and recover," explains Leah Barron, RD, a registered dietitian and certified personal trainer

in New York City.

Limited inflammation can be helpful for preventing injury, too. "I like to think of the mild inflammation we see post-workout as a 'fire drill' of sorts," Barron says. "This is the immune system's opportunity to get in a practice run and maintain efficiency, so when a real injury occurs, it knows exactly what to do to get the healing process started right away."

**IT'S POSSIBLE TO HAVE TOO** much of a good thing, though. A 2020 systematic review in the journal *Frontiers of Physiology* found that intense sweat sessions 30 minutes or longer can either lead to enough chronic inflammation to increase the risk of injury or potentially impair the immune system. The researchers defined *intense* as workouts that raise your maximal heart rate (the upper limit of what your cardiovascular system can handle during physical activity) above 76 percent, the Centers for Disease Control and Prevention–defined window for vigorous exercise. "In other words, too much exercise may be so anti-inflammatory as to induce immunosuppression," says Taylor. "Or people who participate in too much exercise may be susceptible to chronic inflammation due to stress or lack of sleep, rather than exercise itself."

That's not great, seeing as chronic inflammation can open a Pandora's box of problems. In the short term, inflammation can lead to fatigue and mood disturbances. In the long term, it can contribute to atherosclerotic processes and metabolic dysfunction, contributing to heart disease, diabetes, obesity and cancer.

In terms of exercise, chronic inflammation could lead to muscle loss. A 2017 study published in *Cellular Physiology and Biochemistry* linked higher levels of inflammatory markers to age-related decline in muscle function in elderly participants. And, if left unchecked, chronic inflammation could eventually lead to overtraining syndrome, or OTS. "OTS refers to a state where the amount of recovery between exercise training sessions is inadequate to allow for complete restoration of the individual," says Cornish. The thinking behind OTS is that repeated bouts of exercise without adequate recovery will result in chronic inflammation, which then interferes with the muscles' ability to work or perform at the same intensity as they were previously—meaning you're ultimately backsliding.

It also just won't be comfortable. "There will generally be muscle pain—especially on movement or palpation—and altered function, meaning you won't be able to perform exercise tasks as well," says Cornish. "Generally, most exercise-induced muscle damage and the associated inflammatory reaction will subside in 48 to 72 hours after very strenuous or long duration activity. If it persists for longer than that, there may have been some muscle damage that is more serious."

Also worth noting is that inflammation does not always have an immediate effect. Delayed-onset inflammation is entirely possible when you're overdoing it, which does not look the same for everyone. It could entail not taking enough time for recovery and rest, or going from zero to 60 in terms of intensity. So maybe you work out every day for a week without taking a rest day, or you go from running three miles a day to running a half marathon, with no training in between.

"You can go along just fine for three or four months, and there may be some very subtle signs, like your heart rate might start to increase a little bit," says Taylor. "You might start feeling a little more fatigued, stressed and irritable, and you may not be sleeping well, but you're probably not going to notice those things. And then, boom: You suddenly hit that real, overtrained, probably overstressed immune system–compromised world."

The good news is that your walking habit and yoga practice likely aren't to blame. "Certain types of workouts are more likely to trigger inflammation than others," says Barron. "For example, weight lifting is going to cause more of an inflammatory response than walking. Having said that, in order to

continue to elicit the body's inflammatory response, which allows for growth and repair of muscle tissue, we have to continually introduce new and more challenging stimuli." As a result, Barron says, pushing yourself in your workout of choice, be it running more miles, lifting heavier weights or contorting yourself into more challenging yoga positions, is essential for making progress, despite the risk.

There's no easy answer for whether a "sweet spot" exists—that is, a range in which you're working out to the point of triggering the beneficial inflammation, but not so hard that it becomes chronic or harmful. "It was long thought that the sweet spot was moderate-vigorous exercise that met guidelines of 150 minutes per week, but recent studies have established that even light-intensity exercise can have significant and sometimes even greater benefits," says Taylor.

Most important in hitting that happy medium is progression, she says, "since every individual is starting from a different spot in terms of inflammation and needs to progress through intensities and durations of exercise with sufficient time to acclimate to the load." If you've run a few half-marathons, haven't been injured and are relatively healthy, then yes, a marathon is a realistic goal. It's even more important when you're talking about strength or resistance training. "With cardio you're naturally limited, right? If you don't run, it's really hard to go out and run five miles. Your cardiovascular system is going to stop you, because you just don't have the aerobic capacity," Taylor says. "But with resistance training, you can overdo it pretty quickly, and the signal that you've overdone it, like the delayed-onset muscle soreness, doesn't come until 24 to 48 hours later." Since you don't have the built-in stoppers with resistance training that you do with cardio, progression can be that much more important.

Also, don't forget to check in with yourself and take stock of how you feel during and after a workout. "Trainers stress strong communication with their clients," says Barron. "We ask questions throughout the session like 'How difficult did that feel?' and 'How many more reps do you think you could have done?' in order to gauge the difficulty of the exercise and how taxing it is on your body."

You can also ask yourself basic, subjective questions about to your relationship with the workout in question, Taylor suggests. Are you genuinely enjoying your workout? Do you feel happy and energized afterwards? Are you dedicated but not obsessed—meaning you're not sacrificing other things in life for the sake of your workout? "There's no real tracking device for that subjective experience," she points out.

It's also important to remember that exercise doesn't happen in a vacuum. "There is a lot of individuality in how people respond even to chronic inflammation," says Taylor. "Increasingly with marathon runners and endurance athletes, we're recognizing it's not just the exercise itself—it's everything else. So if you want to do long-term, high-level endurance training, which we know comes with a dose of potential inflammation, you need to really manage sleep, stress, diet and all those accompanying things if you want to be able to do so in a healthy way." Think of it as having a budget for your stressors: If your primary stressor is going to be exercise, then you limit the other ways that chronic inflammation can set in. Here's how to do that.

**TAKE YOUR REST DAY** This should go without saying, but recovery is essential. "Generally, the higher the intensity of exercise you are doing or the longer the duration of the exercise you are completing, the longer periods of recovery it may require," says Cornish. "Less intense forms of exercise, known as active recovery, may be needed to allow for full recovery and for performance benefits to be accrued over time. Essentially, it's all about balancing the amount of exercise you complete with adequate recovery from that exercise."

Though it may feel discouraging not to be hitting the weight rack on a given day, you're still actively building muscle even if you're foam rolling or doing some light stretching on a mat. In fact, that 2020 systematic review in the journal *Frontiers of Physiology* found that maximum benefits are achieved when you pair moderate exercise or vigorous exercise with appropriate rest periods.

**ENJOY FISH MORE** A fish-heavy diet can go a long way in mitigating inflammation, thanks to the natural sources of omega-3 fatty acids. "We have this kind of inflammatory cascade that happens, and certain molecules that can sort of block that cascade from flowing from the top of the chain downstream," says Michelle Babb, RD, a dietitian in Seattle. "Omega-3 fatty acids will block that flow of inflammatory cytokines."

**LOAD UP ON VEGGIES AND FRUIT** Plants are one of the most powerful sources of inflammation-regulating nutrients. Start with dark leafy greens. "Kale, chard and collard greens have omega-3 and tend to have a lot of vitamin K, too, which is also very anti-inflammatory," explains Babb. The same goes for beta-carotene—think squash, carrots and yams. It's an antioxidant that can neutralize the oxidative stress caused by inflammation, which is how "it can turn down the volume of inflammation," Babb says. She's also a fan of magnesium, which can be found in root vegetables, beans, nuts and seeds, as well as vegetables and fruit that still have the skin on. (Put down that peeler!) "Magnesium is strongly associated with less inflammation, and it's particularly important for people who tend to exercise or overexercise and get muscle soreness," says Babb. Not only does it help relax the muscles, but a magnesium supplement in the evening can help promote better-quality sleep, as well.

**SLEEP SOUNDLY** The value of sleep often gets underestimated, but it's critical to helping your body repair. "There are four separate stages of sleep that you move through during a sleep cycle, and as your body move moves through each one of those, very unique and distinct things happen—relaxation happens, committing things to memory happens, and a lot of deep muscle recovery and repair functions happen—but your body needs to be relaxed enough to have the capacity for the peripheral nervous system to perform those functions," Taylor explains. "So when we don't get enough sleep, we simply don't have enough sleep cycles to achieve that."

Moreover, when your sleep is poor quality—meaning you're waking often or tossing and turning—you can't get into the deeper sleep cycles, which are critical for repair, recovery, and the reduction of inflammation. Ultimately, it's a matter of both quality and quantity of sleep. ●

# EAT TO KEEP INFLAMMATION AT BAY

Fight chronic inflammation and stay strong with these healthy recipes that highlight foods known for their anti-inflammatory properties.

## Curried Cauliflower Pitas with Cilantro-Mint Sauce

**ACTIVE:** 40 minutes
**TOTAL:** 40 minutes
**EQUIPMENT:** Grill basket, heavy-duty foil

*We use the grill to get a nice char on the cauliflower before stuffing it into pitas, and for crisping up the sandwiches. If you don't have a grill basket, you can place the cauliflower directly on the grates; just be careful when flipping so you don't lose any in the cracks.*

- **½ cup fresh cilantro leaves and tender stems**
- **¼ cup fresh mint leaves**
- **1 scallion, sliced, green and white parts separated**
- **4 tablespoons extra-virgin olive oil, divided**
- **2 tablespoons lime juice**
- **2 tablespoons water**
- **½ teaspoon salt, divided**
- **4 cups cauliflower florets (about 1-inch)**
- **1 tablespoon curry powder**
- **¼ teaspoon ground turmeric**
- **1 15-ounce can no-salt-added chickpeas, rinsed**
- **2 tablespoons low-fat plain yogurt**
- **2 6-inch whole-wheat pita breads, halved**

**1.** Place a grill basket on the grill; preheat to medium-high.
**2.** Combine cilantro, mint, scallion greens, 2 tablespoons oil, lime juice, water and ¼ teaspoon salt in a mini food processor. Process until smooth. Set aside.
**3.** Combine cauliflower, curry powder, turmeric and the remaining 2 tablespoons oil and ¼ teaspoon salt in a large bowl. Transfer the mixture to the grill basket. Cook, stirring occasionally, until the cauliflower is tender, about 10 minutes.
**4.** Meanwhile, mash ¾ cup chickpeas and 2 tablespoons of the reserved cilantro sauce in a medium bowl until almost smooth. Stir yogurt into the remaining cilantro sauce.
**5.** Return the cauliflower to the large bowl and stir in the remaining ¾ cup chickpeas and scallion whites. Spread the mashed chickpeas inside each pita half. Using about ¾ cup for each, divide the cauliflower mixture among the pita halves. Wrap each stuffed pita in heavy-duty foil. Grill until heated through, 3 to 5 minutes. Serve with the yogurt sauce.

**SERVES 4:** 1 PITA HALF & 1½ TBSP. SAUCE EACH
**CAL** 349, **FAT** 16G (SAT 2G), **CHOL** 0MG, **CARBS** 42G, **TOTAL SUGARS** 5G (ADDED 0G), **PROTEIN** 11G, **FIBER** 9G, **SODIUM** 522MG, **POTASSIUM** 617MG.

## Roasted Salmon with Spicy Cranberry Relish

**ACTIVE**: 30 minutes
**TOTAL**: 30 minutes
**TO MAKE AHEAD**: Refrigerate relish (Step 3) for up to 1 day.
**EQUIPMENT**: Parchment paper

*This ruby-red relish gets refreshing crunch from apple and celery. It's also delightful alongside a roast chicken or pork loin.*

- 2½ **pounds skin-on salmon fillet**
- 2 **cloves garlic, peeled and chopped**
- 1½ **teaspoons kosher salt, divided**
- ½ **teaspoon whole black peppercorns, cracked**
- 1 **lemon, zested and cut into wedges**
- 2 **tablespoons extra-virgin olive oil, divided**
- 2 **teaspoons Dijon mustard**
- 2 **cups cranberries, fresh or frozen (8 ounces)**
- 1 **small shallot**
- 1 **serrano pepper, seeded**
- 1 **medium Granny Smith apple, peeled and finely diced**
- 1 **stalk celery, finely diced**
- 1 **tablespoon balsamic vinegar**
- 2 **tablespoons chopped fresh parsley, divided**

**1.** Preheat oven to 400°F. Line a rimmed baking sheet with parchment paper.
**2.** Place salmon on the prepared pan. Mash garlic, 1 teaspoon salt, peppercorns and lemon zest into a paste with a fork or a mortar and pestle. Transfer to a small bowl and stir in 1 tablespoon oil and mustard. Spread on the salmon. Bake until the flesh flakes easily with a fork, 10 to 15 minutes.
**3.** Meanwhile, pulse cranberries, shallot and serrano in a food processor until finely chopped. Transfer to a medium bowl and stir in apple, celery, vinegar, 1 tablespoon parsley and the remaining 1 tablespoon oil and ½ teaspoon salt.
**4.** Sprinkle the salmon with the remaining 1 tablespoon parsley and serve with the relish and lemon wedges.

**SERVES 8:** 4 OZ. SALMON & ⅓ CUP RELISH EACH
**CAL** 229, **FAT** 9G (SAT 2G), **CHOL** 66MG, **CARBS** 8G, **TOTAL SUGARS** 4G (ADDED 0G), **PROTEIN** 29G, **FIBER** 2G, **SODIUM** 452MG, **POTASSIUM** 603MG.

## Scallion-Ginger Beef & Broccoli

**ACTIVE**: 30 minutes
**TOTAL**: 30 minutes

*Whip up a chef-quality stir-fry at home. This one packs in more vegetables and nearly halves the calories of what you would find in a restaurant.*

- ⅓ cup reduced-sodium tamari or soy sauce
- ¼ cup low-sodium chicken broth
- 2 tablespoons brown sugar
- 2 tablespoons cornstarch, divided
- 1 pound sirloin steak, thinly sliced
- 3 tablespoons peanut or canola oil, divided
- 6 cups broccoli florets
- ½ cup sliced scallions, plus more for garnish
- 1 tablespoon finely grated ginger
- 1 teaspoon finely grated garlic
- 2 cups cooked brown rice
- Crushed red pepper for garnish

**1.** Whisk tamari or soy sauce, broth, brown sugar and 1 tablespoon cornstarch in a small bowl. Toss steak with the remaining 1 tablespoon cornstarch.
**2.** Heat 2 tablespoons oil in a large flat-bottom wok or cast-iron skillet over medium-high heat. Add the steak and cook, stirring once, until browned, about 4 minutes. Transfer to a clean plate.
**3.** Add the remaining 1 tablespoon oil and broccoli; cook, stirring occasionally, until slightly tender, about 2 minutes. Stir in scallions, ginger and garlic; cook, stirring, until fragrant, about 30 seconds. Whisk the tamari mixture and add it, along with the beef, back to the pan; cook until the sauce thickens, about 1 minute.
**4.** Serve over brown rice and with crushed red pepper, if desired.

**SERVES 4:** 1 CUP BEEF AND BROCCOLI & ½ CUP RICE EACH
**CAL** 440, **FAT** 16G (SAT 4G), **CHOL** 59MG, **CARBS** 43G, **TOTAL SUGARS** 9G (ADDED 7G), **PROTEIN** 30G, **FIBER** 4G, **SODIUM** 741MG, **POTASSIUM** 781MG.

## Butternut Squash Soup with Apple Grilled Cheese Sandwiches

**ACTIVE**: 30 minutes
**TOTAL**: 45 minutes
**TO MAKE AHEAD**: Refrigerate soup (Steps 1–2) for up to 3 days.

*Layering apple slices into grilled cheese sandwiches adds crunch to a favorite soup dipper. And creamy butternut squash soup with ginger, cumin and turmeric is a nice change of pace from grilled cheese's usual partner, tomato soup. Serve the duo for a comforting and easy weeknight dinner for the family. The soup keeps well in the fridge, so save leftovers for lunch or dinner later in the week.*

- **2 tablespoons grapeseed oil or coconut oil, divided**
- **1 cup chopped onion**
- **2 tablespoons minced fresh ginger**
- **1 teaspoon ground cumin**
- **1 teaspoon ground turmeric**
- **¼ teaspoon cayenne pepper, plus more for garnish**
- **5 cups cubed (1-inch) peeled butternut squash**
- **1 15-ounce can light coconut milk, divided**
- **2 cups low-sodium no-chicken broth or chicken broth**
- **1 small apple, thinly sliced, divided**
- **¾ teaspoon salt**
- **1 tablespoon lime juice**
- **4 slices whole-wheat country bread**
- **1 cup shredded smoked Gouda or Cheddar cheese**
- **Ground pepper for garnish**

**1.** Heat 1 tablespoon oil in a large saucepan over medium heat. Add onion and ginger; cook, stirring, until starting to soften, about 3 minutes. Add cumin, turmeric and cayenne; cook, stirring, for 30 seconds. Add squash, coconut milk (reserve 4 tablespoons for garnish, if desired), broth, half the apple slices and salt. Bring to a boil. Reduce the heat to maintain a simmer and cook, stirring occasionally, until the squash is tender, about 20 minutes. Stir in lime juice. Remove from heat.

**2.** Puree the soup in the pan using an immersion blender or in batches in a blender. (Use caution when blending hot liquids.)

**3.** Divide ½ cup cheese between 2 slices of bread. Top with the remaining apple slices, cheese and bread. Heat the remaining 1 tablespoon oil in a large nonstick skillet over medium heat. Add the sandwiches and cook until lightly browned on both sides and the cheese is melted, about 2 minutes per side. Cut in half. Garnish the soup with the reserved coconut milk, more cayenne and ground pepper, if desired.

**SERVES 4:** 1½ CUPS SOUP & ½ SANDWICH EACH
**CAL** 419, **FAT** 23G (SAT 11G), **CHOL** 26MG, **CARBS** 43G, **TOTAL SUGARS** 10G (ADDED 0G), **PROTEIN** 13G, **FIBER** 8G, **SODIUM** 827MG, **POTASSIUM** 622MG.

EatingWell

**Editor-In-Chief** Jessie Price
**Creative Director** James Van Fleteren

# Eating for Strength

**Editorial Director** Kostya Kennedy
**Creative Director** Gary Stewart
**Director of Photography** Christina Lieberman
**Editor** Courtney Mifsud Intreglia
**Art Director** Wendy Johnson
**Writers** Ashley Abramson, Karen Asp, Mallory Creveling, K. Aleisha Fetters, Rozalynn S. Frazier, Joyce Hendley, Laurie Herr, Emily Joshu, Tula Karras, Danielle Kosecki, Cindy Kuzma, Hallie Levine, Amanda Loudin, Amanda MacMillan, Deanna Pai, Aviva Patz, Holly Pevzner, Lauren Wicks
**Copy Editor** Tracy Guth Spangler
**Reporter** Ryan Hatch
**Associate Photo Editor** Steph Durante
**Production Designer** Sandra Jurevics
**Premedia Trafficking Supervisor** Ryan C. Meier
**Premedia Imaging Specialist** Paige E. King
**Color Quality Analyst** Heidi Parcel

**MEREDITH PREMIUM PUBLISHING**
**Vice President & Group Publisher** Scott Mortimer
**Vice President, Group Editorial Director** Stephen Orr
**Vice President, Marketing** Jeremy Biloon
**Director, Brand Marketing** Jean Kennedy
**Associate Director, Brand Marketing** Bryan Christian
**Senior Brand Manager** Katherine Barnet

**Editorial Director** Kostya Kennedy
**Creative Director** Gary Stewart
**Director of Photography** Christina Lieberman
**Editorial Operations Director** Jamie Roth Major
**Manager, Editorial Operations** Gina Scauzillo

**Special thanks** Brad Beatson, Rachelle Laliberte, Samantha Lebofsky, Kate Roncinske, Laura Villano

**MEREDITH NATIONAL MEDIA GROUP**
**President** Catherine Levene
**President, Consumer Products** Tom Witschi
**President, Meredith Digital** Alysia Borsa
**EVP, Strategic & Business Development** Daphne Kwon

**EXECUTIVE VICE PRESIDENTS**
**Chief Revenue Officer** Michael Brownstein
**Digital Sales** Marla Newman
**Finance** Michael Riggs
**Marketing & Integrated Communications** Nancy Weber

**SENIOR VICE PRESIDENTS**
**Consumer Marketing** Steve Crowe
**Consumer Revenue** Andy Wilson
**Corporate Sales** Brian Kightlinger
**Foundry 360** Matt Petersen
**Product & Technology** Justin Law
**Research Solutions** Britta Cleveland
**Strategic Planning** Amy Third
**Strategic Sourcing, Newsstand, Production** Chuck Howell

**VICE PRESIDENTS**
**Brand Licensing** Toye Cody, Sondra Newkirk
**Business Planning & Analysis** Rob Silverstone
**Finance** Chris Susil
**Strategic Development** Kelsey Andersen
**Strategic Partnerships** Alicia Cervini

**Vice President, Group Editorial Director** Stephen Orr
**Chief Digital Content Officer** Amanda Dameron
**Director, Editorial Operations & Finance** Greg Kayko

**MEREDITH CORPORATION**
**Chairman & Chief Executive Officer** Tom Harty
**Chief Financial Officer** Jason Frierott
**Chief Development Officer** John Zieser
**President, Meredith Local Media Group** Patrick McCreery
**Senior Vice President, Human Resources** Dina Nathanson
**Senior Vice President, Chief Communications Officer** Erica Jensen

**Vice Chairman** Mell Meredith Frazier

# Photo Credits

**Front cover** (food and fitness concept): Nadine Greeff/Stocksy
**Front cover** (healthy ingredients on table): New Africa/Shutterstock
**Back cover** (clockwise from top): Africa Studio/Shutterstock; Westend61/Getty Images; istetiana/Moment/Getty Images

**Page 1:** Delmaine Donson/E+/Getty Images
**Pages 2-3:** Poberezhna/Shutterstock
**Page 5:** Drazen Zigic/iStock/Getty Images
**Page 6:** Lumina/Stocksy

**FOODS THAT FUEL**
**Pages 8-9:** Nadine Greeff/Stocksy **Page 11:** BONNINSTUDIO/Stocksy **Page 12:** OatmealStories/RooM/Getty Images **Page 15:** Artem Evdokimov/Shutterstock **Page 16:** DeanDrobot/iStock/Getty Images **Page 17:** Claudi Kessels **Page 19:** Jay Mid/Addictive Creative/Offset by Shutterstock **Page 20:** Arx0nt/iStock/Getty Images **Page 21:** 5second/iStock/Getty Images **Page 23:** Stanislaw Pytel/DigitalVision/Getty Images **Pages 24-25:** Thomas Barwick/DigitalVision/Getty Images **Pages 26-29:** Claire Benoist/The Licensing Project (2) **Page 31:** Aja Koska/E+/Getty Images **Page 33:** naturalbox/iStock/Getty Images **Page 34:** Cavan Images/Getty Images **Page 35:** Kristin Duvall/Stocksy **Pages 36-37:** Blaine Moats **Page 38:** Emulsion Inc. **Page 39:** Erin Kunkel **Page 40:** Devon O'Brien **Pages 41-42:** Blaine Moats (2) **Page 43:** Allison Miksch

**GETTING STRONGER**
**Pages 44-45:** The Good Brigade/DigitalVision/Getty Images **Page 46:** wragg/E+/Getty Images **Page 49:** KPS/iStock/Getty Images **Pages 50-51:** Westend61/Brand X Pictures/Getty Images **Page 52:** Prostock-Studio/iStock/Getty Images **Page 53:** Morsa Images/DigitalVision/Getty Images **Page 54:** Antonio_Diaz/iStock/Getty Images **Page 55:** Tracy Walker **Pages 56-57:** Rawpixel/iStock/Getty Images **Pages 58-59:** gilaxia/E+/Getty Images **Pages 60-61:** PeopleImages/E+/Getty Images **Pages 62-65:** Tom Corbett (16) **Pages 66-69:** Anthony Cunanan/Gallery Stock (14)

**REST AND RECHARGE**
**Pages 70-71:** Jasmina007/E+/Getty Images **Pages 72-73:** nesharm/iStock/Getty Images **Pages 74-75:** Tero Vesalainen/iStock/Getty Images **Page 77:** Syda Productions/Shutterstock **Page 79:** Prostock-Studio/iStock/Getty Images **Pages 80-81:** Leigh Beisch (2) **Page 82:** Andrea Mathis **Page 83:** Leigh Beisch **Page 85:** Ashley Barker/Offset by Shutterstock **Pages 86-87:** PeopleImages/E+/Getty Images **Pages 88-89:** Ilona Titova/iStock/Getty Images **Page 90:** Jason Donnelly **Page 92:** Leigh Beisch **Page 93:** Blaine Moats **Page 94:** Brie Passano **Page 96** (clockwise from top left): Con Poulos/Offset by Shutterstock; David Sacks/The Image Bank/Getty Images; Joanna Wojewoda/Offset by Shutterstock; Alan Shapiro/Stocksy

# Muscle Soothers

Foods containing anti-inflammatory compounds can ease post-workout aches.

**BY KERRI-ANN JENNINGS, MS, RD**

If you've been exercising more, and especially if you've been upping your strength-training regimen, you may be suffering from the aches and pains of having overdone it at the gym. Making sure your workout is challenging without overdoing it is one way to prevent muscle soreness. But research also points to certain foods and beverages that can aid in muscle recovery, helping to avoid and minimize the soreness. Here are a few favorites.

**BLUEBERRIES**
Research done in New Zealand suggests that the antioxidants in blueberries may help ward off muscle fatigue by mopping up the additional free radicals that muscles produce during exercise.

**TART CHERRIES AND POMEGRANATES**
Researchers found that people who drank an ounce of concentrated cherry juice twice daily for 10 days bounced back faster from their workout (an intensive leg-resistance training session on day eight) than those who skipped the juice. The reason: The anti-inflammatory and antioxidant properties in tart cherries—and other fruit juices, such as grape and pomegranate—essentially act as natural NSAIDs (nonsteroidal anti-inflammatory drugs, such as ibuprofen and aspirin), reducing exercise-induced muscle damage.

**GINGER**
Ginger is rich in inflammation-fighting compounds such as gingerols, which may reduce the aches of osteoarthritis and soothe sore muscles. In a 2010 study, people who took ginger capsules daily for 11 days reported 25 percent less muscle pain when they performed exercises designed to strain their muscles compared with a similar group taking placebo capsules. Another study found that ginger-extract injections in more than 200 participants helped relieve osteoarthritis pain in the knees.